Imparting the Blessing

by

William T. Ligon, Sr.

Web:

www.thefathersblessing.com

Imparting the Blessing to Your Children
10th Edition
ISBN 1-86327-00-9
Copyright © 1989 by
William T. Ligon Sr.

All Scripture quotations are from the Authorized King James Version (KJV).

Cover designed by Stafford Burney.

Published by
The Father's Blessing
PO Box 2480
Brunswick, GA 31521

(912) 267-9140

To My Family

Dorthy Jean, John, William and Kim,
And the grandchildren:
Will, Wyatt, Sarah Camille, Mary Lee, and Anna Catherine

- who have taught me how to bless

Host a Seminar

Pastor Ligon and his son John are each available to conduct seminars on The Power of the Spoken Blessing or Character Building through the Ten Commandments. Blessing seminars usually go for four session, Sunday a.m. and p.m. and Monday and Tuesday evenings. Contact us at: 912-267-9140.

Start A Small Group

Sign up today to partner with us to direct small groups in a study of the power of the blessing. Those desiring to lead a small group will need a recommendation from their pastor and approval from The Father's Blessing, office. You may contact us in the following manner:

Online - thefathersblessing.com
Phone - 912-267-9140
Mail - PO Box 2480 Brunswick, GA 31521

Contents

Foreword

Chapter 1 page 1
THE VALUE OF YOUR CHILD

Chapter 2 page 9
BLESSING GOD'S PEOPLE - A BIBLICAL OVERVIEW

Chapter 3 page 16
WHY BLESS YOUR CHILDREN

Chapter 4 page 22
LEARNING FROM THE PATRIARCHS

Chapter 5 page 30
THE REDEMPTIVE POWER OF THE BLESSING

Chapter 6 page 39
HOW TO BLESS YOUR CHILDREN

Chapter 7 page 46
JACOB FOUND HIS BLESSING

Chapter 8 page 61
HOW TO BREAK THE CURSE

Chapter 9 page 70
PLANNING A SPECIAL BLESSING

Additional Resources page 88

FOREWORD

God planned for life to be imparted to His children through the spoken blessing. It is a duty of parents to follow the plan established by the patriarchs to insure the success of the blessing. The Old Testament fathers expected their blessings to be fulfilled in the lives of their children. That same expectation can rest in the hearts of parents who accept the challenge to bless their own children.

Jehovah God used the spoken blessing personally to impart divine favor to His people. He verbally blessed Adam and Eve (Genesis 1:28), Abraham (Genesis 12:1-3) and Jacob (Genesis 32:24-32). Jesus began His three year training program with His disciples by speaking a series of blessings over their lives (Matthew 5:1-16).

Isaac verbally blessed his sons Jacob and Esau (Genesis 27). Jacob later blessed Joseph by speaking blessings over Joseph's sons, Ephraim and Manasseh (Genesis 48). Moses taught Aaron and his sons to speak blessings over God's people each time they assembled the people together (Numbers 6:22-27).

The record is endless throughout the Bible of blessings being spoken over the people of God. Yet, for some reason the Church has neglected the Biblical commands to bless. We owe a debt to Judaism for preserving the traditions of family blessings. This author feels that the success of Jewish children can be traced back to the faithfulness of their fathers to bless them.

It is expected that this practical study will encourage parents to begin to bless their children. Outstanding results are anticipated as homes begin to enjoy the benefits of the blessing.

Pastor William T. Ligon, Sr. Brunswick, Georgia

Chapter I

THE VALUE OF YOUR CHILD

"Lo, children are an heritage of the
LORD: and the fruit of the womb is
his reward."
(Psalm 127:3)

No one can place a value on your children. They are priceless gifts from the Lord, described in the Bible as "olive plants round about thy table." (Psalm 128:3b). King David was shown that his covenant children would sit upon his throne forever (Psalm 132:12c). That promise of blessing from God was fulfilled in the birth of Jesus Christ and continues to be realized in the lives of many children today.

Satan sees covenant children as the greatest threat to his plans. He does not want children to come under the covenant blessings of God. That can be seen in his efforts to destroy men like Moses and Jesus during their infancy. If Satan had succeeded in destroying them, he would have blocked Gods plans for man's redemption. Seeing God's plan for the deliverance of the children of Israel embodied in the life of the child Moses, he prompted Pharaoh to kill all the firstborn males (Exodus 1 & 2). Knowing that eternal redemption rested in the life of the baby Jesus, Satan prompted Herod to slay all the male children under two years of age (Matt. 2:16). What if he had succeeded in cutting, off those two children? Redemption of mankind would have been aborted. Failing to impart to children the blessings of God helps to assure Satan that he can foil

1

God's plans for them. The Lord has something special that He wants to accomplish through children. He has placed them in the care of parents to nurture and train for the fulfillment of that purpose. Satan knows that and he will do everything in his power to prevent parents from imparting life to their children through spoken blessing.

The following lessons will give great hope to parents who are concerned about the spiritual health of their children. God has given a very clear plan in the Bible for imparting blessings to children. Parents who complete this study will have a command of Scriptural principles which will help them effectively impart blessings to their children.

Children - A Sign of the Covenant

God's covenant blessings spoken over His people included the promise of offspring. His first act after creating Adam and Eve was to bless them and say, "Be fruitful, and multiply, and replenish the earth, and subdue it: and have dominion over the fish of the sea, and over the fowl of the air, and over every living thing that moveth upon the earth." (Genesis 1:28). Here we have the first Scriptural evidence that God's blessing was intended to bring forth new life, encouraging growth and rulership among His people.

Noah and his sons received the same blessing, from God following the flood. Genesis 9:1 says, "And God blessed Noah and his sons, and said unto them, 'Be fruitful, and multiply, and replenish the earth.'". Noah and his sons could not be fruitful and multiply without having children. God made it clear to them that the bringing forth of offspring would be a part of the covenant He was establishing with them. "And I, behold, I establish my covenant with you, and with your seed after you;" (Genesis 9:9).

God's covenant blessing spoken to Abraham began to express the redemptive nature of the covenant which He was establishing; "And I will make my covenant between me and thee, and will multiply thee exceedingly." (Genesis 17:2), God's plan of perpetuating His covenant through children was first introduced to Abraham. Abraham's faith in God's promise rested on the confidence that his own child was an integral part of God's plan. Isaac was his covenant child. The Abrahamic promise included the promise of offspring and the promise of blessing for Abraham. "And in thy seed shall all the nations of the earth be blessed;" (Genesis 22:18). The multiplication of offspring was an important part of God's covenant with both Isaac (Genesis 26:4) and Jacob (Genesis 28:14).

The promises in the Davidic covenant are similar to those God made with Abraham. In II Samuel 7:11-12, David is promised offspring through whom God will establish the house of David forever. David was conscious of the fact that it was the favor of the Lord that would bring about the blessings upon his household. "Therefore now let it please thee to bless the house of thy servant, that it may continue for ever before thee: for thou, 0 Lord God, hast spoken it: and with thy blessing let the house of thy servant be blessed for ever." (11 Samuel 7:29). The future of Gods people extended far beyond the life of David, resting on the concept of covenant children coming after him.

It is through children that God plans to impart the redemptive benefits of the covenant. The promise of children is common to all the covenants God has made with man. Each time you look at your children remember that they are a sign that God has not nullified His promise. The prophet Malachi taught that the sign that the covenant blessings were being poured out upon the people of God was that

3

"the heart of the fathers were turned to the children, and the heart of the children to their fathers…." (Malachi 4:6).

Gods covenant plan for redemption has not changed. He will continue His work through children who have been blessed and confirmed in the faith. The Lord has ordained that parents will perpetuate His redemptive work by imparting blessing to their children and teaching them to do the same for their children. Thus God has placed great value upon the life of children. They are His plan for tomorrow, that through them the life of Jesus Christ can be given to the world.

Educating Parents to Bless

Satan is doing everything, in his power to cut the children off from the blessings of God, just as he attempted to do so by plotting the death of Moses and Jesus Christ. His efforts are again falling short as parents learn the value of their children in the Kingdom of God. Parents educated in Gods plan for imparting the blessing will learn to bless daily, expecting the favor of God to rest upon their children.

The patriarchs of the Old Testament went to great length to impart blessings to their children. Jewish fathers have continued the tradition, speaking special blessings over their children weekly. Their children have enjoyed the benefits of such commitment to God's command to bless. That is how the benefits of God's favor are passed on from one generation to another.

Unfortunately, the Christian church has, for the most part, failed to develop a serious practice of blessing children. That should be very pleasing to Satan. If he can distract parents from those responsibilities or keep them ignorant of the power resting in the blessing, he can interrupt the plan of God for raising up a covenant people for Himself.

Blessing In The New Testament

Blessing in the New Testament falls under two main categories having to do with redemption and the imparting of Divine favor. Paul says in Galatians 3:13-14 that "Christ hath redeemed us from the curse of the law,....that the blessing of Abraham might come on the Gentiles through Jesus Christ; that we might receive the promise of the Spirit through faith." A special blessing comes to those who receive Jesus Christ as Lord of their lives by faith. The curse which prevented people from receiving this blessing was broken when Jesus was crucified. Now any person who calls upon the name of the Lord can be saved, receiving the blessing God promised Abraham. That is the first and most vital meaning of blessing in the New Testament.

The second form of blessing mentioned in the New Testament is the one which has been neglected and, sometimes, never taught in the Christian churches. It is that blessing which commands the attention of this study. In Mark 10: 16 we are told, "And He took them (children) up in His arms, put His hands upon them, and blessed them." All the synoptic gospels record this incident, catching the interest of discerning parents to the action of Jesus. Why did Jesus lay His hands on children and bless them? What did He say to them? We can believe that He said some of

5

the same things that Jewish fathers have said to their children for centuries when they blessed them. He did it because the spoken blessing imparted special favor from God upon the children. If that is not the case, then why did Jesus perform a ritual which has no purpose?

Jesus saw merit in speaking blessing over those He loved. Luke's gospel records an interesting event in the ministry of Jesus. In Luke 24:50-51 Luke says, "And He led them out as far as Bethany, and He lifted up His hands, and blessed them. And it came to pass, while He blessed them, He was parted from them, and carried up into heaven." The last act of Jesus toward His disciples was to speak a blessing over them. As He was speaking that blessing with His hands lifted after the fashion of the priests, He rose into the clouds. You can almost see him rising with His hands out stretched speaking life, peace and success over His people.

The apostle Peter carried the principle of blessing over into his teaching. In I Peter 3:8-9 he says, "Finally, *be ye* all of one mind, having compassion one of another, love as brethren, *be* pitiful, *be* courteous: Not rendering evil for evil, or railing for railing: but contrariwise blessing; knowing that ye are thereunto called, that ye should inherit a blessing." We are called to give blessings. That is the thesis of this study. In the next two chapters we will learn what the blessing is all about, how it is imparted and the benefits one can expect from receiving it.

Review – Chapter 1

1. Which people in your family are the greatest threats to Satan's future plans? _____

   _____

2. What people are found to be a part of all Old Testament covenant promises God made with man? _____

   _____

3. What will help to assure Satan that he can abort the plan of God for your children? _____

   _____

4. God's first act after creating Adam and Eve was to _____

   _____them (Genesis 1:28).

5. Malachi taught that the sign that the covenant blessings of God were being poured out on His people was that _____

   _____

   _____(Malachi 4:6).

6. The benefits of God's favor are passed on from one generation to another by means of _____

   _____

7. Blessing in the New Testament falls under two categories: (1) Redemption and (2) _____

   _____

8. Why did Jesus lay hands on children and bless them? _____

_____

_____(Mark 10:16)

9. What was the last act of Jesus before He ascended into heaven?

_____(Luke 24:50-51)

10. What must we do to inherit a blessing according to Peter? _____

_____

_____(I Peter 3:8-9)

Answers found at end of book

8

Chapter 2

BLESSING GODS PEOPLE
A BIBLICAL OVERVIEW

"On this wise ye shall bless the children of Israel..." (Numbers 6:23)

God's first act after creating Adam and Eve was to speak a blessing over them. "So God created man in His own image... And God blessed them, and God said unto them, 'Be fruitful, and multiply...'" (Genesis 1:27-28). Thus, God gave special grace to man by imparting the power of fruitfulness to him through the blessing. That action of God is only the first of many Biblical references where the practice of blessing was observed.

Genesis 9:1 records blessing of fruitfulness which God imparted to Noah and his sons after the flood. The thought of fruitfulness is again present when God says to Abraham, "I will make my covenant between me and thee, and will multiply thee exceedingly." (Genesis 17:2). The Lord had already told Abraham that He would bless him (Genesis 12:2b) and that he would be a blessing to all the families of the earth.

Melchizedek king of Salem spoke a blessing over Abraham following his defeat of Chedorlaomer and the kings who were with him. Serving Abraham bread and wine, the symbols of the body and blood of Jesus Christ, Melchizedek verbally declared, "Blessed be Abram of the most high God...which hath delivered thine enemies into thy hand." (Genesis 14:19-20a). Hebrews 7:1 notes the

9

importance of the act of blessing in which Melchizedek included the giving of bread and wine to Abraham. Hebrews 7:7 develops the experience further by saying, "And without all contradiction the less is blessed of the better". Melchizedek imparted divine favor to Abraham through the spoken blessing. In return, Abraham gave one tenth of all he had earned to Melchizedek.

Rebekah received a spoken blessing from her family when she prepared to leave to be married to Isaac. They said, "Thou art our sister, be thou the mother of thousands of millions, and let thy seed possess the gate of those which hate them." (Genesis 24:60b). Ruth and Boaz were blessed by their people just before their marriage. In Ruth 4:11, the people imparted the blessing by saying, "We are witnesses, The Lord make the woman that is come into thine house like Rachel and like Leah, which two did build the house of Israel: and do thou worthily in Ephrathah, and be famous in Bethlehem." When Jesus was born in Bethlehem that blessing was fulfilled.

The concept of blessing takes on greater significance in chapter 27 of Genesis. Here, Isaac made preparation to speak blessing over his oldest son before he died. The occasion was of such importance that it included a meal in which the elderly patriarch was served his favorite dish before speaking the blessing. The significance of the blessing is also evidenced by the fact that the mother Rebekah devised a skillful plan to insure that the blessing was spoken over her younger son, Jacob. The power of the spoken blessing was confirmed by the fact that it was said to be irrevocable once delivered (Genesis 27:33). The strength of the blessing was confirmed when Isaac spoke a second blessing over Jacob before he left to seek a wife (Genesis 28:1-3). When we add to those two blessings a third one spoken by the Lord Himself over Jacob during a dream, we have strong evidence to support the authority of the first blessing spoken by Isaac (Genesis 28:13-15).

Jacob's personal desire to be blessed demonstrates the importance he placed upon the spoken blessing. Genesis 32:24-30 graphically illustrates the value Jacob placed on the spoken blessing. After wrestling with the Angel of the Lord all night, he declared, "I will not let thee go except thou bless me."(v.26) the text goes on to say, "And he blessed him there." (v.29b). God later gave more support to the life and ministry of Jacob by speaking an additional blessing over him (Genesis 35:9-12). The Lord imparted to him grace to be fruitful, multiply and see his children become kings to the nations. He also gave Jacob a blessing to succeed materially. Jacob impressed upon Joseph the importance of the blessing by referring to the blessing God Almighty spoke over him at Luz in the land of Canaan (Genesis 48:3).

The 48th chapter of Genesis is a touching example of the value the Hebrew family placed upon children. Joseph stood his two sons, Ephraim and Manasseh before his father Jacob, who then proceeded to speak a blessing over them. Verse 15 indicates that Joseph was blessed as his father began to speak the blessing over his sons. When Jacob said, "In thee shall Israel bless, saying, God make thee as Ephraim and as Manasseh:" (Genesis 48:20), he instituted a practice of blessing children which is still observed today. Those tender moments with Joseph and his sons were followed with a formal gathering of the twelve sons of Jacob, during which time Jacob spoke blessings over all of them before he died.

Jacob's blessings spoken to his twelve sons in Genesis 49 constitutes a series of tribal blessings in which all the members of each tribe received the blessing given to their leader. A similar ritual was observed by Moses just before his death as recorded in Deuteronomy 33.

The Priestly Blessing

God's concern for the welfare of His people is highlighted in Numbers 6:22-27 when He commanded Moses to teach Aaron and his sons to bless the sons of Israel. He then gave Moses a three-part blessing which He required to be spoken over His people each time they assembled together. Known among Jewish people as the "High Priestly Blessing", it was expected to invoke the blessings of the Lord Himself when it was spoken. In Leviticus 9:22 Aaron lifted his hands toward the people and blessed them. The words Aaron spoke were the same as those found in Numbers 6:24-26:

> The Lord bless you, and keep you;
> The Lord make His face shine on
> you; And be gracious to you;
> The Lord lift up His countenance on
> you; And give you peace.

The positive effect of the community blessing was to be felt throughout the twelve tribes as they settled in the land of promise. In like manner, blessings which parents speak over their family should affect every area of family life. David said: "For the sake of my brothers and my friends, I will now say, 'may peace be within you'. For the sake of the house of the Lord our God, I will seek your good." (Psalm 122:8-9). David did seek the good of his people as demonstrated by his desire to bless them in the name of the Lord after he had brought the ark back into Jerusalem. (II Samuel 6:18).

The New Testament offers evidence that the practice of blessing was common among the Jewish people and was continued in the life of the church. Jesus Christ began His three year training program with His disciples with a series of blessings. The beatitudes listed in Matthew 5 are a series of blessings accompanied by corresponding rewards. The disciples eventually experienced everything the Lord spoke over them in the beatitudes.

Jesus went further in expressing the idea of blessing in Matthew 5:13 and 14. He said to His disciples, "Ye are the salt of the earth" and "Ye are the light of the world." At that time, the disciples were neither of those things, yet Jesus said that they were. Some of them had serious character defects which would take time to correct. They were unregenerated men who would not know the joy of being born again until after the crucifixion and resurrection of Jesus Christ. Many of their old habits, such as Peter denying Jesus and cursing during Jesus trial, were still unbroken. In spite of all that, Jesus was able to bless them by declaring them to be effective witnesses in the world. The act of speaking that kind of success over their lives was a blessing which became a reality.

Jesus again demonstrated His confidence in the power of the blessing when He blessed children. Mark 10:16 states that "He took them up in His arms, put his hands upon them, and blessed them." What did Jesus say to the children when He blessed them? We can expect that He spoke encouragement to them about their futures, adding the words of Jacob in Genesis 48:20b, "God make thee as Ephraim and as Manasseh." Most certainly He spoke life and encouragement to them. The same would be true of the content of Jesus' speech when He lifted up His hands and blessed the people as He ascended into heaven (Luke 24:50). His commitment to the principle of blessing could not be more intensely declared and less understood than in His words in Luke 6:28, "Bless them that curse you, and pray for them which despitefully use you."

The same attitude is carried forward in the writing of the Apostle Paul when he says, "Bless them which persecute you:

13

bless, and curse not." (Romans 12:14). Peter gave added support to the concept of blessing when he encouraged the believers to not return evil for evil, or insult for insult and he said they were to give a blessing instead; for they were called for the very purpose that they might inherit a blessing.

Such evidence in both the Old and the New Testaments leaves little doubt that God has planned for the blessing to be used to impart life to those who receive it. Parents who learn to impart the blessing to their children on a regular basis can hope to see very positive results in their lives. As one father in New England said, "My children have seen so much good coming to them since I began to speak blessing over their lives that they would not think of leaving for school without receiving a blessing."

Review – Chapter 2

1. How was the power of fruitfulness and productivity imparted to mankind? _____

2. How did King Melchizedek impart divine favor to Abraham?

   _____

   _____(Genesis 14:19-20)

3. Hebrews 7:6-7 says that the lesser is _____ by the greater and that the greater _____

   _____ from the lesser.

14

4. What did Rebekah's family do for her before she married Isaac?

_____

_____(Genesis 24:60b)

5. Once delivered, the blessing is said to be _____
   (Genesis 27:33)

6. Jacob wrestled all night with a man to receive a blessing from
   him. Who was he? _____

   _____(Genesis 32:24-30)

7. The blessing God gave for Moses and Aaron to speak over His
   people is called _____

   _____

8. What was the spiritual condition of the disciples when Jesus
   called them "salt" and "light"? _____

   _____ (Matt. 5:13-14)

9. What did Paul say that we should do for people who curse us? _

   _____

   _____(Romans 12:14)

10. Peter said that, instead of returning evil for evil, we are to _____

    _____

    _____(I Peter 3:8-9)

Answers found at end of book

15

Chapter 3

Why Bless Your Children?

And they shall put my name upon
the children of Israel; and I will bless
them."
(Numbers 6:27)

Blessing children accomplishes much more than merely encouraging them in their daily lives. That was seen by the parents of Stephen who was not passing in school. Stephen had failed the Seventh grade the previous year. Now he had brought home his first report card with all failing grades for his second year around in the same grade. The attentive parents had held conferences with the school officials, punished Stephen and even attempted to encourage change by offering rewards. They were careful to see that Stephen was in "Sunday School" and church each week. In spite of all their sincere efforts, nothing was working for them.

In desperation they appealed to their pastor for prayer. Perhaps God would do something to turn Stephen's life around. When the pastor offered to teach them the Biblical principles of blessing, they readily accepted. Soon they were applying the Biblical plan of blessing to Stephen's life, laying hands on him daily and speaking success into every area where he had failed. Stephen's attitudes began to change. He completed the Seventh grade level that year with high scores and moved on to the next level where he continued to succeed. Similar cases to that of Stephen have been experienced where parents have learned the value of blessing their children, devoting the time necessary to learn how to bless. Their diligence in imparting blessing has paid off for their children.

God obviously had something special in mind for His people when He commanded Moses and Aaron to bless the children of Israel. There is no wasted motion in the activities of God. He does not institute rites as a matter of form. There is a purpose behind every movement and command of God. Every activity He institutes produces life at a higher level when it is observed.

Practicing the high priestly blessing in Numbers 6:22-27 was the vehicle God obviously desired to use so that He could bless His people. First, God expected Aaron and his sons to obey His command and speak the priestly blessing over the people. Then God said that, as they invoked His name, He would be present in the blessing to impart blessing to them. "And they shall put my name upon the children of Israel; and I will bless them."

Aaron and his sons were to invoke (engaged, put into action, the life that flows from the name of God) and God would be present, imparting life to those who received the spoken blessing. **That is the way God chose to impart something of Himself to His people**. Jesus continued to use the rite of blessing to impart life to His followers. The Apostle Peter says that believers are to do the same thing (I Peter 3:9). Even the experience of being born again comes about through the spoken blessing. Romans 10: 8-10 says, "But what saith it? The word is nigh thee, even in thy mouth, and in thy heart: that is, the word of faith, which we preach; That if thou shalt confess with thy mouth the Lord Jesus, and shalt believe in thine heart that God hath raised Him from the dead, thou shalt be saved." The person believes the Word and speaks life over himself by confessing that Jesus is Lord. What he speaks in faith becomes

17

a reality in his life. He blesses himself and the blessing of God is invoked in the power of the Holy Spirit to give the person new life in Jesus Christ. **The fact is that everything man ever receives from God he receives by the spoken word. Even faith comes by hearing the Word of God**.

An old Jewish fable tells of a rabbi who questioned God one day about the high priestly blessing. "Why should I bless your people when you can do it so much better?" he asked. God replied that He commanded the rabbi to bless, but that He was present in the blessing, imparting life to His people. Parents who understand that **God is present in the blessing when they speak it** over their children, will be more faithful to engage in the practice of speaking blessing over them every day.

The high priestly blessing in Numbers 6:24-26 was invoked at the end of worship when the community was about to be dismissed. The people were to carry the benefits of the blessing with them into their homes and their work. **The effect of the blessing was to be felt in every area of their lives - their character, their community relationships and their relationship to God**.

The building of godly character is one of the benefits which can be expected when children receive the blessing imparted to them by their parents. So it was with Stephen who was mentioned earlier. Stephen began to receive new motivation to apply himself to his studies. Instead of being distracted and slothful, he became alert and attentive to the important matters in his life. His old problem had nothing to do with any learning disability. Stephen's character changed when his parents began to impart life to him through the blessing - and so did his grades.

God spoke of blessing to Abraham within the context of the established covenant He was making with him. The Lord's first words to Abraham in Genesis 12:1-3 relate **the blessing to covenant practices**. God relates to mankind on the basis of covenant. All of God's activity in history is expressed through covenant. **God guaranteed His promises with Abraham through covenant**. Thus, when the Lord says, "And I will make of thee a great nation, and I will bless thee, and make thy name great; and thou shalt be a blessing' (Genesis 12:2), He was relating the promised blessings to the covenant He was making with Abraham.

Jesus also related blessing to covenant when He said in Luke 22:29, "And I appoint unto you a kingdom, as my Father hath appointed unto me;". The word, "appointed", stems from the word for covenant in the Greek. Therefore, Jesus is saying that just as the Father had covenanted to Him a kingdom, so He was covenanting to His disciples a kingdom. That kingdom would be one in which the blessings of Father God would be imparted to His children. **Jesus came in covenant with the Father to pass on those blessings to His disciples in covenant with them**. He accomplished that fact and **released blessing through His crucifixion**.

Paul expands on the concept of covenant and blessing in Galatians 3:13-14, when he says, "Christ hath redeemed us from the curse of the law, being made a curse for us: for it is written, Cursed is every one that hangeth on a tree: "**That the blessing of Abraham might come on the Gentiles through Jesus Christ; that we might receive the promise of the Spirit through faith**."

Parents who commit themselves to begin to bless their children can do so with confidence knowing that they are in covenant with Father God through the blood of Jesus Christ. God has established the bringing forth of offspring as a part of every covenant He has made with man - from Adam to Abraham, Moses and King David. The recognition that children are a gift of God and

19

a sign that God keeps covenant with every generation helps to give confidence to parents when they prepare to impart blessings to their children on a regular basis. **God never planned for children to be deprived of the blessing** which was to be imparted to them through their parents and the religious leaders of their community.

    Recognizing the blessing as Gods way of bringing the covenant into active play upon the lives of their children is one of the great responsibilities of parents. Knowledge of the power of the blessing and God's plan for using it will encourage concerned parents to bless their children. As parents then understand how the future of their children often hangs upon, their willingness to bless, they will devote themselves to learning how to impart the blessing. "I never realized just how powerful the blessing could be," one mother said, "...until I began to speak blessing over my hyperactive child. I see changes taking place as I bless him every day with peace, self-control and unselfish love for others."

Review – Chapter 3

1. What vehicle did God give to Moses and Aaron so that divine favor could be imparted to the children of Israel? _____

_____

_____(Numbers 6:22-27)

2. How was the name of God to be put on (invoked over) the children of Israel? _____

_____(Numbers 6:27)

3. Who actually did the blessing as Aaron spoke it over the people?

_____

4. Everything that mankind ever receives from God comes by means of _____

5. How does a person experience the new birth? _____

_____

_____(Romans 10:8-10)

6. Faith comes by _____

_____

_____(Romans 10:17)

7. God's first words to Abraham in Genesis 12:1-3 relate the blessing to _____

_____

8. In Luke 22:29 Jesus relates covenant to _____

_____

9. In Galatians 3:13-14 Paul relates redemption to _____

_____

_____

10. What will cause parents to bless their children regularly? _____

_____

_____

Answers found at end of book

Chapter 4

LEARNING FROM THE PATRIARCHS

"By faith Isaac blessed Jacob and
Esau concerning things to come. By
faith Jacob when he was a dying,
blessed both the sons of Joseph; and
worshiped, leaning upon the top of
his staff."
(Hebrews 11:20-21)

Isaac and Jacob's practice of imparting blessing to their
children was of such importance that it found its place in the
hallmark of faith in Hebrews, chapter 11. The Holy Spirit attests to
the importance of blessing by acknowledging its place within the
family of believers. Informing themselves about the use of blessing
by the fathers of the Bible will help parents bring rich rewards into
the lives of their children. Parents are blessed with the satisfaction
of seeing their children enjoy the benefits that come from the
blessing.

It should be said that imparting blessings is not a sure
guarantee that children will respond positively or that there will not
be any failures. Jesus took twelve men and imparted blessings to
them, accompanied by teaching from the scriptures. Although they
studied three years with Jesus, He was successful with only eleven
of them. The twelfth one betrayed Him. King David was a man who
knew how to bless, yet one of his sons, Absalom, stood at the gate
of the city and turned the people against his father. However, it can

be said that the success rate of the fathers of the Bible was much higher than the families in the churches today. For the most part, the church has failed to teach the people to bless one another. Where families have recovered the lost art of imparting the blessing, they have seen remarkable results in the lives of the children. "My seven year old daughter was a bed-wetter", one father relates. "We tried everything from punishment to rewards. She did not respond to us or to medical help. Then the Word of God began to heal her. My wife and I heard about the power of the blessing. After studying, the principles, we began to speak life over our daughter. We blessed her with self-control and confidence. We blessed her with a new self-esteem and assurance that she was loved and appreciated by the family. Her bed wetting soon stopped and her self-respect increased greatly. She never wet the bed again." Everyone enjoys hearing the story of a person who was healed by the Word of God. But it is evident that even the Bible does not promise one hundred percent success with the blessing. On the other hand, that should not discourage parents from imparting blessings to their children. Failures among children are reduced to a minimum when parents are faithful to bless them with the Word of God.

Isaac's Training

Isaac is known as the child of promise. He was aware that something special was about to happen when Abraham went to offer him as a sacrifice before God (Genesis 22). Isaac was certainly old enough to understand what was happening because his father laid the wood for the sacrifice on his shoulders for the last part of their journey together (v.6). He heard the Angel of the Lord remind

Abraham that God's blessings upon his seed (children) were a part of His covenant plan for Abraham. He witnessed the faithfulness of God in providing a ram as a substitute for his own life. The knowledge that Isaac gained from those experiences and the lessons he received from his father prepared him to bless his own children when he was old.

Making Preparation To Bless

Isaac took the initiative himself to prepare for a special blessing to be spoken over his son Esau. He understood that **the blessing had deep significance in the life of his son**. Therefore he said, "Prepare a savory dish for me such as I love, and bring it to me that I may eat, so that my soul may bless you before I die." **Isaac wanted to be in the right frame of mind when he spoke the blessing because his words would significantly affect the future of his son**. He was about to speak forth a blessing, which, in his society, would serve as a last will and testament.

The preparation taken to prepare for the blessing is of vital significance in preparing parents for the blessing, over their children today. **Isaac's entire life was filled with blessing rites which formed character in him and provided direction for his life**. That is not so for the average church member today. The absence of family traditions which provide insight into the purpose of the blessing requires that parents who wish to bless take time to study and understand the principles of blessing given in the Word of God. Those **parents who gain the conviction** that the blessing will enrich the lives of their children **will consistently use the blessing to strengthen their lives**.

In Genesis 28:1 Isaac blessed Jacob the second time, including in the blessing a charge that he would not marry an unbeliever. **Marriage is a covenant which greatly influences the faith of the marriage partners**. The patriarchs took care to insure that their children married within the limits of the covenant established with Jehovah God. When Esau wanted to rebel against his parents out of spite, he married unbelievers. (Genesis 28:8). **Parents should be careful to begin early to bless their children with godly wives and husbands**. The way they word their blessing will greatly affect the decisions the children make later when they choose their life partners. Such blessings from the parents should come out of the deep convictions of their own hearts. If they do not believe what they are saying, they will not have much power when they impart the blessing.

Avoiding Isaac's Folly

There is a flaw in Isaac's understands of blessing which deserves attention. Isaac suffered conflict in his spirit when he prepared to bless his sons because he ignored an important word from the Lord. In Genesis 25:21-23, the Lord spoke in prophecy to his wife, Rebekah, telling her that she was going to have twins and that the older would serve the younger. When Isaac prepared to speak the blessing of the first-born over his son, he should have remembered the Word of the Lord. His partiality for his first-born, Esau, caused him to overlook the prophecy and prepare to speak the first-born blessing over Esau. Only through the action of Rebekah was Isaac able to avoid being disobedient to the Lords command.

25

Giving more attention to the will of the Lord could have helped Isaac prepare his sons for the pronouncement of the last will and testament which was given in the form of a blessing. He could have spoken the first-born blessing over Jacob and another blessing over Esau without provoking Esau to wrath. **Parents who plan to use the blessing should prepare early, planning something special for each child in their family. Care should be taken to avoid partiality in anything that is said during the blessing**.

Letting Grandparents Bless

Jacob's experience in his old age brings to light the place of grandparents in imparting the blessing. Looking again at Genesis 48, Jacob, who was very weak, gathered his strength and sat up in his bed when Joseph entered with the two grandsons. Jacobs attention to them, claiming them as his own, serves as a source of encouragement to **grandparents to consider the responsibility of imparting blessing to all their grand children**. The place of grand parents in the lives of children cannot be overstated. One family prepared all the grandchildren for a special visit before the grandparents. The grandchildren were lined up beginning with the oldest. The grandparents were seated side-by-side in two chairs to allow them to extend their hands to bless the children. When the younger children saw their older cousins kneel before their grandparents and bow their heads to receive a blessing, they followed in line and did the same. Before the blessings were finalized with the youngest, the presence of the Lord was manifested in the room,

26

moving the children, parents and grandparents into a time of special reverence before the Lord. Grandparents have the capacity to bless with great anointing.

The High Priestly Blessing

The high priestly blessing given in Numbers 6:24-26 highlights the importance of the entire family or community of believers participating in times of blessing. Aaron and his sons were taught to bless the sons of Israel by saying to them, "The Lord bless thee, and keep thee". **The wording of the blessing is an acknowledgment that it comes from God. The purpose is to bless the people with protection from the evil of the world. The blessing of care and protection should be spoken over the children and the family daily.**

The second part of the blessing says, "The LORD make his face shine upon thee, and be gracious unto thee;". **The face of God is the personality of God expressed in loving favor to man.** Sometimes, God turned His face away in disfavor and chastisement. David prayed, "Make Thy face to shine upon Thy servant:" (Psalm 31:16a). The face of the Lord shining upon children results in special blessings being bestowed in their lives. **Imparting that blessing could only result in good for your children.**

The final part of the blessing states, "The LORD lift up His countenance upon thee, and give thee peace." (Numbers 6:26). That **speaks of a manifestation of power upon the people, resulting in peace on their lives. It is the sum total of all the good which the Lord does for His people.** This blessing will release special favor upon the children, making it easier for them to experience success in their lives.

All three parts of the priestly blessing should be spoken over children at some time during a blessing service. Peter says that we are a "chosen generation, a royal priesthood..." (I Peter 2:9a). Learning to impart the blessing to children and others for whom we are responsible is an excellent way to begin to function as priests. When it is done in faith, it should release many blessings upon those who receive the blessing.

<u>Review – Chapter 4</u>

1. How important were Isaac's and Jacob's practice of blessing? _
   _____
   _____

2. Who was known as the child of promise in the Old Testament? _
   _____(Genesis 22)

3. God taught Abraham that His blessing on Abraham's seed was part of God's _____ for Abraham. (Genesis 22:6)

4. Who took the initiative in preparing the blessing for Jacob and Esau? _____(Genesis 27:1)

5. When should parents begin to bless their children with godly wives and husbands? _____

6. What was Isaac's folly which we should be careful to avoid? __

_____

_____

7. God's plan for Esau and Jacob was that the _____
should serve the _____ (Genesis 25:21-23)

8. Who saved Isaac from imparting the first-born blessing to the
older son Esau? _____ (Genesis 27)

9. What Old Testament passage emphasizes the importance of
grandparents blessing their grandchildren? _____

_____

10. What passage of Scripture highlights the importance of families
participating in times of blessing together? _____

_____

Answers found at end of book

Chapter 5

THE REDEMPTIVE POWER
OF THE BLESSING

"And he blessed them that day,
saying, In thee shall Israel bless,
saying, God make thee as Ephraim
and as Manasseh: and he set Ephraim
before Manasseh."
(Genesis 48:20)

When we look at the Scriptures to understand the power
of the blessing, evidence surfaces to show that **God's plan for
blessing is a redemptive one**. It is made, as we shall see, on the
principle of **divine substitution** in which the older son lays down
his rights to the birthright in favor of his younger brother. The entire
experience is ex-pressed in prophetic terms as it points to the time
**when Jesus Christ comes in response to man's cry for a blessing
from God. God hears the cry of the sinner for mercy and blesses
him by imparting the blessing of His first-born, Jesus Christ,
to the sinner**. The effect of the blessing of salvation is that God
substitutes the life of Jesus for the death of the sinner. The sinner,
who deserves to die, lives instead. The Savior, who deserves to live,
dies in his place.

When the thought of seeking a blessing for Ephraim and
Manasseh was first introduced in Genesis 48:1, the first-born,

Manasseh, was named first. But when the elderly Jacob spoke of his grandsons, he reversed the order and named the younger Ephraim first (v.5). Joseph then proceeded to place his small sons before his father so that his right hand would fall on the head of Manasseh, the older one, and his left hand would fall on Ephraim's head (v.13). Joseph's plan of having Manasseh receive the blessing of the first-born failed when Jacob extended his hands to speak blessing over the two boys, crossing his arms so that his right hand fell on the head of the younger Ephraim and his left hand fell on the head of the older Manasseh (v.14).

The Right Hand of Blessing

The right hand was considered the hand that imparted the greater blessing. (Jesus Christ is seated at the right hand of the Father in heaven.) Therefore, it displeased Joseph to see his father imparting the greater blessing to his younger son, Ephraim (v.17). He then attempted to move his father's right hand from the head of Ephraim to Manasseh (v. 18). Jacob refused to reverse the position of his hands, **saying that he knew what he was doing** (V.19). Then he proceeded to pronounce a blessing in which he put Ephraim first.

The order in which Jacob blessed his Grandsons was of such vital importance to the act of blessing that **the text calls attention to it: "and he set Ephraim before Manasseh."** (v.20b). Joseph knew the custom of granting the greater blessing to the first-born who, in turn, was expected to become responsible for the tribe when the father died. It was a double-portion blessing in which the older received twice as much inheritance as the younger. The extra inheritance was needed to oversee the responsibilities of the tribe when the father died. It came as a total surprise to Joseph that his father reversed the order of blessing, imparting the greater blessing to the younger.

Jacob blessed Joseph by blessing his sons, causing the firstborn blessing to fall upon him also. Speaking to Joseph, Jacob says, "Moreover I have given to thee one portion above thy brethren..." (v.22). Ruben was actually the first-born of Jacob. His blessing over Ruben formally removed the first-born blessing from him: "Unstable as water, thou shalt not excel", Jacob declared as he blessed Ruben (Gen. 49:4a). Later when Jacob spoke his last blessing over Joseph, he finalized the transfer of the first-born blessing from Ruben to Joseph:

> "The blessings of thy father have
> prevailed above the blessings of my
> progenitors unto the utmost bound of
> the everlasting hills: they shall be on
> the head of Joseph, and on the crown
> of the head of him that was separate
> from his brethren."
> (Gen. 49:26)

Jacob gets Esau's Blessing

Further evidence of the effect of divine substitution upon the blessing is found in the birth of Esau and Jacob. While the twins struggled in Rebekah's womb,__ the Lord said to her, "the elder shall serve the younger__." (Gen. 25:23c The prophecy was fulfilled in the shrewd plan of Rebekah who hastily prepared Isaac's favorite dish, disguised her younger son, Jacob, and sent him before his blind father to receive the first-born blessing. __The strength of the blessing with its legal application__ is found in a part of the blessing which Isaac spoke over Jacob: "be lord over thy brethren, and let thy mother's sons bow down to thee:" (Gen. 27:29b). __Even after the deception was uncovered, Isaac allowed the blessing to stand (v.33), upholding the fact that the younger had received the blessing which belonged to the firstborn__.)

Prophecy Revealed

There are two other passages of Scripture which shed light on the meaning of the blessing imparted to Jacob. They are found in Malachi 1:1-3 and Romans 9:1-16. The people complained in Malachi 1 that God did not love them. "I have loved you, saith the LORD. Yet ye say, Wherein hast thou loved us? Was not Esau Jacob's brother? saith the LORD: yet I loved Jacob, And I hated Esau.. ."(Mal. l:2-3a).

Understanding of God's answer through Malachi is given by Paul in Romans 9. Paul talks about the deep longing in his heart to see Israel saved. He stated that he would be willing to be separated from Christ for the sake of his brothers (v.3). He then recalled the prophecy God gave to Rebekah in Genesis 25 when He said, "The elder shall serve the younger."(v.12). And finally, he referred to Malachi's words when he said, As it is written, Jacob have I loved, but Esau have I hated."(v.13). This Scripture relates salvation to the blessing, given to Jacob.

By using Jacob's experience of receiving the blessing, of the first-born, Paul has identified the relationship between the preferred place in Isaac's blessing, and the preferred status when the sinner receives the life of Jesus Christ in place of punishment for his sins. **The sinner reaches the place that he realizes his lost condition places him in a hopeless state. He appeals to God for deliverance, crying, 'Lord, be merciful to me a sinner." God, in response, reaches into the life of His first-born, Jesus, and takes the blessing from Him to give to the repentant sinner. The new life the sinner receives is the life of Jesus. Jesus, in return, gets Calvary.**

Divine Preference Shown

God shows divine preference when He gives eternal life to a sinner. The sinner deserves to die because of his sins. Jesus, who was without sin, deserves to live. But God sends Jesus to the cross to die in the sinner's place and transfers the life of Jesus over to the sinner. The sinner receives the resurrection life of the firstborn as a blessing. Considered in that light, the words of Paul in Galatians 3:13-14 are replete with revelation: "Christ bath redeemed us from the curse of the law, being made a curse for us: for it is written, Cursed is everyone that hangeth on a tree: That the blessing of Abraham might come on the Gentiles through Jesus Christ; that we might receive the promise of the Spirit through faith." The act of willfully giving up His birthright is reflected in

34

the words of Jesus in Matthew 20:28 when He said, "...**the Son of man came not to be ministered unto, but to minister, and to give his life a ransom for many**." Paul says in Philippians 2:8 that Jesus "humbled Himself, and became obedient unto death, even the death of the cross." One difference between Jesus and Esau is that Jesus willfully released His birthright that it might be given to sinners. Esau resented the substitution and allowed bitterness into his spirit instead of honoring the redemptive plan of God.

Jews Bless Like Father Jacob

The blessing Jacob spoke over Ephraim and Manasseh has been repeated many times through the ages by dedicated Jewish fathers as they imparted blessing to their sons. A part of the blessing includes the words, "May God make you like Ephraim and Manasseh." Using this rite on the Sabbath to impart blessing to their sons, Jewish fathers have repeatedly acknowledged the redemptive plan of God who would impart blessing to all mankind through the Messiah who was to come. Christian literature seems to be almost entirely void of any reference to seeing **the blessing as a redemptive rite which acknowledges God's plan of salvation being imparted to man**. The opportunity is missed to take the principles of blessing and use them for the children. Therefore, a rich heritage has been lost to the church and to children who have seen the opportunity to receive blessings.

Malachi said that the people questioned whether God loved them. The prophecy shows that they were people bound to their circumstances. **They judged God's love by the way God blessed**

them materially. But God placed the appraisal of His love on the basis of divine preference. "Was not Esau Jacob's brother? saith the LORD: yet I loved Jacob…" (Mal. l:2-3a). **That same divine preference occurs with sinners**. Believers often judge Gods love for them by the way He blesses them materially. "But God commendeth His love toward us, in that, while we were yet sinners, Christ died for us." (Romans 5:8). Paul says it is clear that God still shows His love through divine preference. **Jesus crucified at Calvary is the evidence that God loves the believer**.

Each time Jewish fathers have spoken the blessing of Ephraim and Manasseh over their sons, they have declared that preference without realizing its full significance. When parents speak blessings over their children today, they too declare the preference of God for their children. Every child has the right to have that preference spoken over his life many times. **Many children who are in trouble will be released from bondages when the receive blessings**.

Girls in Jewish households receive another blessing which deserves out attention. Each Sabbath, the daughter stands before her parents as the father says, "May the Lord make you like Rachel and Leah, both of whom built the house of Israel." Rachel and Leah brought forth from their households all of the heads of the twelve tribes of Israel. Their sons became heads of state. They were leaders of nations. The words of the blessing come from the book of Ruth in chapter 4:11-12 where a blessing was spoken over Boaz and Ruth by the townspeople. They said, "The LORD make the woman that is come into thine house like Rachel and like Leah, which two did build the house of Israel; and do thou worthily in Ephrathah, and be famous in Bethlehem." That blessing came true to the fullest as Boaz and Ruth became the grandparents of King David and the ancestors of Jesus who was born in Bethlehem. The townspeople did not know how Boaz and Ruth would become famous in Bethlehem. They spoke the blessing. God did the rest.

When parents begin to understand the redemptive power of the blessing, they will take the time to impart blessings to their children on a regular basis. This study is designed to help parents use the principles of blessing to the greatest extent possible. The next chapter will show parents ways they can bless their children, using creativity to help them appreciate the value of the blessings being spoken over them.

Review – Chapter 5

1. Reversing the order of names to name the younger child first, as in Genesis 48, is a _____ expression.

2. Joseph placed his oldest son, Manasseh, so that the _____ Hand of his father Jacob would fall on his head (Genesis 48:13).

3. When Jacob crossed his arms, his right hand fell on the head of the younger _____ (Genesis 48:14).

4. The hand considered to be the one imparting the greater blessing was the _____ hand.

5. How did Jacob bless Joseph? _____

_____

6. Blessing the younger over the older was a shadow or type of the Christian's relationship to God's first-born _____

_____

7. Through the blessing of Abraham, the sinner receives _____
_____ and Jesus receives?

_____

8. When Jewish fathers bless their sons like Ephraim and Manasseh they unknowingly declare the _____ plan of God for mankind.

9. The reversal of blessings, giving the younger the first-born blessing is called divine _____

_____

10. When Jewish girls are blessed, their parents say, May the Lord make you like _____ and _____ who built the house of God.

Answers found at end of book

38

Chapter 6

HOW TO BLESS YOUR CHILDREN

"And all the people departed
every man to his house: and David
returned to bless his house."
(I Chronicles 16:43)

We have seen in this study the principles upon which the blessing is established in the Word of God. Parents should be encouraged by the fact that **the Lord is the one who blesses when they invoke His name over their children**. **Children who receive blessings from their parents on a regular basis will notice the difference in their lives**. It will not be long, until they will ask to be blessed if the parents overlook the responsibility.

There is an old Jewish custom which helps train children to show respect and reverence for the Word of God. Children, who develop a love for the Word and then receive that Word spoken over them in the form of blessing, enjoy spiritual benefits which do not come to everyone. Jewish parents will take a dip of honey and place it on the lips of their small children. As their babies savor the sweet taste of the honey, the parents tell them that the Word of God (Torah) is as sweet as honey and much to be desired. Jewish parents who observe that custom instill in their children a deep love and respect for the Torah which makes it easy for them to receive their blessings.

Visualizing Your Child's Success

When I was a boy, I had a friend who never received blessings from his parents. They were concerned parents who took Robert to church every Sunday to help him learn to live the good life. They were critical of every mistake he made and warned him that if he did not change his ways he would turn out to be a failure in life. Robert became nearly everything his parents warned him he would become. They could never seem to see beyond Robert's immediate attitude or behavior. **Their attitude toward him was controlled by Robert's actions, not their faith**.

Jesus related to people on the basis of **the potential He saw in their lives. He called His unregenerated, untrained disciples the "salt of the earth" and the "light of the world"** (Matthew 5-13-14). **He saw what they would become through the Word He spoke to them daily**. When Jesus told Peter that he would deny Him three times, He prefaced it with the words, "when thou art converted, strengthen thy brethren." (Luke 22:32b). **He could have said, "if you are converted…"**, but **He said "when**. He could have told His disciples that if they stayed with Him long, enough and tried hard enough they might become the salt of the earth and the light of the world. But **Jesus was able to see the possibilities in His disciples. Therefore, He called them "salt" and "light"**. They were already that in the heart of Jesus, so they became what He spoke over them.

Isaac and Jacob related to their sons the same way as Jesus when they blessed them: "By faith Isaac blessed Jacob and Esau concerning things to come. By faith Jacob, when he was a dying, blessed both the sons of Joseph…" (Hebrews 11:20-21).

It was by faith that the patriarchs spoke blessings over their children. They blessed from the heart, expecting all that they said over their children to come to pass. **Parents should pray, asking God to give them the ability to visualize the successful future of their children. With a clear vision of the potential in each child, the blessing can be spoken with authority and confidence.** Since all discipline should be designed to produce good character in children, **correction can be given within the context of blessing.** As the discerning father turned his son over his knees to paddle him, he was heard to say, **"You are a fine boy and this type of behavior has no place in your life."** **That father had the ability to see beyond a temporary failure in his son's character.** The son was fortunate to have a father who knew how to bless even when he was disciplining him. If the parents do not believe in the future of their children, the children's lives will be one up-hill battle after another.

Desiring the Best

Isaac asked Esau to hunt game and prepare his favorite dish so that he could eat it before speaking the blessing. **Having the right attitude is important to imparting the blessing to your children.** Just as discipline cannot be conducted out of a heart full of anger, **blessing cannot come out of a critical attitude.** David said, **"Because of the house of the LORD our God I will seek thy good."** (Psalm 122:9). **Parents should work through their own feelings before they attempt to bless.** Once they reach the point that they "seek" the "good" for their children, they can begin to

41

bless. **That attitude can sometimes be achieved through prayer, or the study of the Holy Scriptures**. Working through this study guide will encourage parents to prepare their souls well before they attempt to bless.

Verbalizing the Blessing

Every blessing in the Bible is a verbal one. Genesis 1:28 says, "And God blessed them (Adam and Eve), and God said unto them…" David said, "For the sake of my brothers and my friends, I will now say, May peace be within you." **The blessing is always a spoken one, not just a desire hidden in the heart** of a parent. **Words have power when they are released**. Loving parents should find it easy to choose effective words to impart blessings to their children. Those who are accustomed to being, very quiet may need to give special attention to developing the art of communication through the spoken word. When God instructed Moses to speak to Aaron and his sons about imparting blessing to the sons of Israel, He said, "**Thus you shall bless the sons of Israel, You shall say to them**:"

Some parents who normally are non-verbal about their faith will demonstrate great ability to express themselves when called upon to bless their children. When I picked up the telephone, the excited voice on the other end of the line said with joy, "Pastor, I must tell you what happened to me today. I was listening to your tapes on Imparting the Blessing, when I suddenly felt remorse that my father could not bless me. I had never heard him pray, read the Bible or express a desire to attend church. Almost at the same moment on the tape, you said that some would think that their parents could not bless them for a lack of spiritual commitment in the parent's life. You went on to say that God would honor their office and that the blessing imparted from them would have a positive effect on the child who received it. I went home immediately and asked my father to bless me. After I explained to him what the blessing was all about, he laid hands on me and spoke the most wonderful blessing I could imagine. Pastor, I feel that I am floating about two feet off the ground." Her father who was normally silent about his faith, had brought the words forth out of a heart full of love for his daughter. We never know what will come out of our mouths when we choose to speak life over our children.

Laying on of Hands

Joseph drew his two young sons very close to his father, Jacob, so that he could lay his hands on the boys. Mark 10:16 says that Jesus "took them (children) up in his arms, put his hands upon them, and blessed them." The church has been faithful to practice the laying on of hands for the ordination of church leaders. In some cases, churches have preserved the work of healing through the laying on of hands. Yet few have taught the parents of the church to lay hands on their children and bless them. The rite is observed in many Jewish homes each Sabbath.

Children should be taught to kneel before their parents in expectation as they lay their hands upon their heads and impart blessing to them. As the hands come to rest upon the children, they will learn to expect God to impart special favor to them.

The Blessing Irrevocable

Paul said in Romans 11:29 that "**the gifts and calling of God are without repentance**." That is, **they are irrevocable**. **The permanency of the blessing spoken in faith gives strength to the children when they receive it**. Isaac confirmed that the blessing, once given, had permanent value in the life of the one who received it. When Esau returned from hunting game and preparing his father's favorite dish, he and his father, Isaac, learned that someone else had already received the firstborn blessing. Upon hearing it, the text says that "Isaac trembled very exceedingly". After inquiring as to whom it was that he had already blessed, Isaac said almost abruptly, "**yea, and he shall be blessed**... (Genesis 27:3). Blessings have great authority in the lives of the children who will receive them. And **no one can take their blessings away if they respect them enough to keep them**.

<u>Review – Chapter 6</u>

1. Jewish parents place a dip of honey on the lips of their small children and tell them the Word of God is as _____ as honey.

2. Parents must _____ success in their children in order to bless them.

3. Jesus related to people on the basis of the _____ _____ He saw in their lives.

4. The Patriarchs blessed their children by _____ _____ (Hebrews 11:20-21)

5. Parents can bless their children and _____ them at the same time.

6. Every blessing in the Bible is a _____ one.

7. Parents who normally are non-verbal about their faith must learn to speak _____ when blessing their children.

8. When blessing, parents must learn to put their _____ on their children blessing them.

9. Children should be taught to _____ a blessing when hands are laid on them.

10. According to Romans 11:29, the gifts of God are _____ _____

Answers found at end of book

45

Chapter 7

Jacob Found His Blessing

John Wesley Ligon

God reveals in Genesis 18:19 that He chose Abraham for the purpose of directing his children and his household after him to keep the way of the Lord by doing what was right and just. That way God would bring about for Abraham the promises He spoke over him. It was important that Abraham taught his children what he learned from the Lord. The welfare of the next generation was on the line. We certainly see Abraham's attitude of wholehearted obedience in Genesis 22 when God told him to sacrifice his beloved son Isaac in the region of Moriah. He immediately made preparations and left.

Abraham's attitude towards obedience, according to Genesis 18:19, makes a point. The lives of his children were a witness to the world of the lessons God taught Abraham because he was faithful to walk it out and pass it on. From that small deduction we know for sure that the Lord taught Abraham the power of imparting blessing. We can see that Isaac walked in God's blessings and blessed his sons just as Jacob did with his sons and grandsons. Had Abraham's children not learned this from their father, they would not have practiced it in such great faith with their own children. (Gen 25:11, 26:12, 48 and 49)

We can look to Abraham's grandson as the example because much is said about him in Genesis. Jacob's life demonstrates the divine fulfillment of spoken blessings. This chapter will briefly outline Jacob's discovery of blessing, his desire to gain it, his development as a result of receiving it, and his determination to walk out a life of faith and obedience to God. Also in the sections labeled "blessings fulfilled" we can see the power and demonstration of God's blessings being applied to Jacob.

Jacob's Discovery (Gen 25:27)

Jacob's understanding of the Lord's blessing was learned from the stories his father and grandfather told as he grew up. He was convinced of God's covenant faithfulness. Therefore, he determined to receive his verbal blessing.

- Genesis tells that Jacob grew up staying around the tents. He spent a lot of time around Abraham and Isaac where as Esau spent much of his time out hunting game.
- Jacob was described as a quiet man and that would make him more prone to listening.
- Abraham lived with him among the tents and impacted his life for 15 years before he died at 175.
- Jacob lived 40 and some say 60 years with his father Isaac before he received the firstborn blessing and left to find a wife at his uncle Laban's home.

He heard

- About God's power, protection, and grace when He delivered Abraham from the power of kings and pharaohs. Gen 12:17 Gen 20:3
- How God had called Abraham to slay Isaac
- Abraham's obedience & Isaac's rescue. Gen 22
- He heard the stories of God making covenants with his grandfather. Gen 12, 15, and 17
- He learned the purpose and power of the spoken blessing God had spoken over Abraham. Gen 12, 15, and 17

- He learned the blessings that Abraham had spoken over his father Isaac.
- The Lord appears to Jacob and confirms the covenant relationship that existed with his father Isaac and grandfather Abraham along with their obedience to Him. This confirmed to Jacob God's approval of his parents and grandparents lives and the lessons that they shared with him.

He saw

- God multiply his father's crops a hundred fold in the midst of a famine. Gen 26:1 & 12
- God protect his parents' lives and marriage from king Abimelech. Gen 26:8
- His father meet with the Lord and the Lord renew His covenant with Isaac. Gen 26:2-6

Certainly Jacob's heart was stirred by these stories to the point of desiring a personal covenant relationship with God where God's favor and blessing became his very own.

Jacob's Desire

Jacob's desire for God's blessing was fueled by what he learned at home. He was moved to the point of taking personal risks to see that he was in the middle of grace. He believed in its value and he would not be left out. Gen 25:29-34, 27, 32:24-26

- He was not the firstborn yet he boldly offered to trade the birthright inheritance of Esau's for a bowl of stew.
- To gain the blessing he risked of losing his life from his angry brother.

- At the risk of receiving a curse from his blind father he masqueraded to gain the firstborn blessing spoken over him.
- The Lord appeared to him on his journey back home from Laban's. Jacob grabs Him and wrestles with Him all night saying that he would not let Him go until he received a blessing.

Isaac spoke blessing in the name of the Lord over Jacob.

(The blessing Jacob received)

27 And he came near, and kissed him: and he smelled the smell of his raiment, and blessed him, and said, See, the smell of my son is as the smell of a field which the LORD hath blessed:

28 Therefore God give thee of the dew of heaven, and the fatness of the earth, and plenty of corn and wine:

29 Let people serve thee, and nations bow down to thee: be lord over thy brethren, and let thy mother's sons bow down to thee: cursed be every one that curseth thee, and blessed be he that blesseth thee. Gen 27:27-37 KJV

- **The dew of heaven** – spiritual blessings of life, strength, and refreshment from God's throne, extending God's authority and life to be rained down on Jacob. Spiritual blessing meant spiritual fruit and character: love, joy, peace, patience, kindness, goodness, faithfulness, gentleness, and self-control.
- **The fatness of the earth** – to bless the health and wealth of

49

his soul and body. All the natural provision he could need would be given in abundance. This more than met the needs of being sustained. He was given abundance described as more than needed (fatness).

- **And plenty of corn and wine**: It goes along with the fatness of the earth so that what he had been given would be sustained and sustained with joy.

- **Let people serve thee and nations bow down to thee**: He was given favor in relationships with neighbors, business acquaintances, and those who ruled and were in authority. It promoted peace and respect.

- **Be lord over thy brethren and let thy mother's sons bow down to thee:** He was receiving the firstborn blessing to accommodate the responsibility of maintaining the household. He would need order and unity for the household to survive and prosper because a divided house would not stand.

- **Cursed be everyone that curseth thee and blessed be everyone that blesseth thee:** An atmosphere of protection and favor was conveyed. The people Jacob would relate to would become aware that they were blessed if they blessed Jacob and they were cursed if they cursed him. That was a make-or-break proposition that wise men would soon figure out.

Jacob received one more blessing from his father Isaac. Rebekah, his mother, was looking out for Jacob's safety because of

Esau's anger and threat. She asked that Jacob travel to her brother's home and marry from their own people and not from the daughters of Canaan. Before Jacob left Isaac spoke this blessing over him saying,

> 28:1 And Isaac called Jacob, and blessed him, and charged him, and said unto him, Thou shalt not take a wife of the daughters of Canaan.
>
> 2 Arise, go to Padan-aram, to the house of Bethuel thy mother's father; and take thee a wife from thence of the daughters of Laban thy mother's brother.
>
> 3 And God Almighty bless thee, and make thee fruitful, and multiply thee, that thou mayest be a multitude of people;
>
> 4 And give thee the blessing of Abraham, to thee, and to thy seed with thee; that thou mayest inherit the land wherein thou art a stranger, which God gave unto Abraham.
>
> Gen 28:1-4 KJV

Jacob's Determination (The fulfillment of Blessing)

Jacob in Genesis 27 finally gets the blessing he longed for. Over his lifetime he faced many hardships that were life-threatening or just plain aggravating, yet God's hand was with him. He grew in the blessing. His new lease on life was bound to the blessing and not in the hardships he faced.

Jacob left home immediately following the blessing. Strangely enough he leaves to go on this 400-mile journey back to Haran with nothing more than the staff in his hand. It seems he would have been given plenty of provisions but he wasn't. What he did have proved life-giving to him. He had the blessing Isaac spoke over him in faith and his staff, the sign of authority that was placed in his hand. Gen 32:10 The first night of his journey the Lord appeared to him in a dream. What happened next is really extraordinary to ponder.

10 And Jacob went out from Beer-sheba, and went toward Haran.

11 And he lighted upon a certain place, and tarried there all night, because the sun was set; and he took of the stones of that place, and put them for his pillows, and lay down in that place to sleep.

12 And he dreamed, and behold a ladder set up on the earth, and the top of it reached to heaven: and behold the angels of God ascending and descending on it.

13 And, behold, the LORD stood above it, and said, I am the LORD God of Abraham thy father, and the God of Isaac: the land whereon thou liest, to thee will I give it, and to thy seed;

14 And thy seed shall be as the dust of the earth, and thou shalt spread abroad to the west, and to the east, and to the north, and to the south: and in thee and in thy seed shall all the families of the earth be blessed.

15 And, behold, I am with thee, and will keep thee in all places whither thou goest, and will bring thee again into this land; for I will not leave thee, until I have done that which I have spoken to thee of. Gen 28:6-15 KJV

God opened Jacob's eyes so he could see what he had strived so hard to gain. God showed him what he had received from his

52

father. The dream was a vision of God's blessing in a nutshell. The Lord's angels would deliver the blessings, minister to Jacob, and report back. This provision and way of life was real. Jacob had believed it but now he could see it. It was the same provision that Jesus spoke about to Nathanael when he said,

Verily, verily, I say unto you, Hereafter ye shall see heaven open, and the angels of God ascending and descending upon the Son of man. John 1:51 KJV

Jacob's Vision Of God's Blessing

- Vs. 12, the gate and path was open
- Vs. 12, the angels were ascending and descending on it ready to
  o Bringing the dew of heaven (spiritual gifts and refreshing)
  o The fatness of the earth
  o An abundance of corn and wine
    - The Lord stood at the top of the ladder showing that He was going to do the blessing.
    - Vs. 13, God affirmed to Jacob that He was the God of his father. God was true to the words that Jacob's father and grandfather obediently spoke over him.
    - Vs. 14, Jacob was going to receive the wife and family that he was going to his uncles to find.
    - Vs. 15, Jacob was shown that God's safety and presence went with him wherever he went and he was given the assurance that God would accomplish all that was spoken over him.

Jacob made a vow that if the Lord would keep him safe on the journey and give him food to eat and clothes to wear that the Lord would be his God. He also vowed to honor Him by tithing 10 percent of what God gave him. Gen 28:20-22

Jacob arrived safe at his uncle's home and stayed for the next 20 years. He helped Laban by shepherding his flocks. A month later Laban asked him what his wages should be. Jacob said he would work seven years for his youngest daughter Rachel. The years seemed like nothing to him and when they were complete he was ready to marry. He was given Leah instead since she was the oldest. A week later he was given Rachel and she also became his wife. He agreed to work another seven years for her. Gen 29:14-30

During the second seven years Jacob worked for Laban, Jacob fathered eleven boys and one girl. Gen 29:32-30:22 God blessed him with quite a large family in a short period of time. Likewise, Laban's flocks prospered under Jacob's management. Gen 30:27 At the end of his fourteen year obligation Jacob wanted to return to his father's house to begin building an inheritance for his own family. Laban, however, was eager to keep Jacob around because the little he had when Jacob arrive had greatly multiplied.

Blessings fulfilled

- Jacob arrived at his uncle's home safe.
- Jacob gets married to Rachel and Leah and in seven years fathered eleven boys and one girl fulfilling the blessing the Lord and his father spoke over him for marriage and children.

- Jacob agreed to marriage in exchange for his labor. Laban blessed Jacob by giving him a home, food, safety, and his daughters as the agreed wage. Laban's flocks grew and he became prosperous. (God blessed Laban because he blessed Jacob.) Gen 30:27

Laban asked Jacob to stay and once again negotiate his wages. Jacob offered a plan that God had shown him in a dream. Laban accepted. Gen 31:10-12 The Lord also reminds Jacob of the previous dream he had of the ladder and the Lord at the top of the ladder. He also reminds Jacob of his vows. It may have seemed to Jacob like the blessing was delaying but the Lord was reminding him that it was not. God was still in charge and He was about to abundantly deliver Isaac's first blessing. Gen 31:13 Gen 31:43

Later, God tells Jacob that it is time to go back to his father's house. During the six-year period Jacob worked for Laban, Laban cheated him. Yet Jacob's wealth grew and Laban's dwindled. Gen 31:4-9 Because Laban's attitude towards Jacob had changed for the worst, Jacob flees for home when Laban was away shearing his sheep. This is discovered and Laban gathers a band of men to confront Jacob. He intended to do Jacob harm and take away his family and all his possessions. God intervenes with a strong rebuke to Laban and peace is made between the men. Jacob loses nothing. Gen 31:19-52

More Blessings fulfilled

- Before Laban asks Jacob to stay and work longer, the Lord appears to Jacob and reminds him of the dream he had fourteen years before. {1)The ladder with the angels ascending and descending and the Lord standing at the top, and 2)the vow he had made.} God was showing Jacob his blessing of "the fatness of the earth" was coming.
- God blessed Jacob by giving him a divine plan to increase the herds that belonged to him. Jacob obeyed, starting with few, and at the end of six years was incredibly wealthy.
- Laban changed the wages that Jacob was to receive ten times, but no matter how he arranged it Jacob's flocks grew and his dwindled
- Because the new bargain for wages was violated by Laban's cheating, Laban was losing his flocks. God cursed him for cursing Jacob.
- Jacob became afraid of Laban and foolishly left without saying goodbye. Laban in his anger caught up with Jacob intending to do him harm. God in a dream intervened for Jacob. In a warning the Lord rebuked Laban telling him not to harm Jacob. God kept Jacob safe.

Jacob is then brought word that his brother Esau is on his way to meet him with a large band of armed men. Jacob is afraid and devises a plan to pacify his brother. He splits his possessions into two bands and sends ahead valuable gifts of various livestock, donkeys, camels, sheep and the like to offer as gifts in order to pacify his brother. He stays back while this is happening and prays to the Lord, crying out for his own safety. After the prayer he makes his own preparations to survive the peril he now faces. He is alone and the Lord appears to him. Jacob grabs Him and will not let go of Him demanding, "I will not let thee go, except thou bless me".

26 And he said, Let me go, for the day breaketh. And he said, I will not let thee go, except thou bless me.
27 And he said unto him, What is thy name? And he said, Jacob.
28 And he said, Thy name shall be called no more Jacob, but Israel: for as a prince hast thou power with God and with men, and hast prevailed.
29 And Jacob asked him, and said, Tell me, I pray thee, thy name. And he said, Wherefore is it that thou dost ask after my name? And he blessed him there.
30 And Jacob called the name of the place Peniel: for I have seen God face to face, and my life is preserved. Gen 32:26-30 KJV

Jacob, now Israel, meets his brother Esau and finds grace. They show affection for each other and are reconciled. Gen 33:4 Jacob moves back to his homeland, builds an altar to worship the Lord, and settles in with all the abundant provisions with which the Lord has blessed him. He settles in Shechem. Gen 33:18-20 There he and his family go through many trials that end with Jacob feeling threatened by his neighbors. The Lord tells him to go back to Bethel. He returns safely and the Lord appears to him again to pronounce a blessing over him.

9 And God appeared unto Jacob again, when he came out of Padan-aram, and blessed him.

10 And God said unto him, Thy name is Jacob: thy name shall not be called any more Jacob, but Israel shall be thy name: and he called his name Israel.

11 And God said unto him, I am God Almighty: be fruitful and multiply; a nation and a company of nations shall be of thee, and kings shall come out of thy loins;

12 And the land which I gave Abraham and Isaac, to thee I will give it, and to thy seed after thee will I give the land.

13 And God went up from him in the place where he talked with him. Gen 35:9-13 KJV

Jacob set up an altar and worshiped the Lord who had appeared to him. As they moved on to Ephrath, Rachel gave birth to his twelfth son Benjamin and died from a difficult labor. The nation of Israel is born in the conception of his twelve sons.

When we see Jacob again he is well along in years and he is again restored to Joseph, who he thought was dead. Joseph saves his family, Egypt, and the surrounding nations from the effects of a seven-year famine that devastates the world. The family is brought to Egypt and given the best land to live in and pasture their animals. Gen 47:27 The final passages before the Lord takes him on home to heaven speak of the blessings that he bestows on his grandsons Menassah and Ephraim. Gen 48 He also speaks blessing over all his sons that were appropriate to them in Genesis 49. After this blessing he drew his feet up into his bed, breathed his last breath, and was gathered to his people.

Jacob lived an amazing life filled with struggles, difficulties, blessings, and restored joy. God kept him and fulfilled the blessings He and Isaac spoke. The blessing Jacob received was fulfilled in the midst of ordinary and extraordinary moments in his life.

Jacob's Children's Blessings

- When Jacob and his family traveled God put a fear of them in the hearts of the surrounding people so they would not attack this wealthy family to harm or rob them Gen 35:5
- Jacob was kept safe during the famine and lost none of his family or property
- Jacobs's son was used to bless the people of the world at the time by administering a food program for pharaoh during a famine. All the nations of the earth were blessed by him fulfilling a spoken blessing.
- Jacob blesses Joseph's two grandsons.
- Jacob's last act testified once more to the authentic work of the verbal blessing in the kingdom of God. Blessing is recorded as the last act of Jacob before he rested and God took him home.

Review – Chapter 7

Answers found at end of book

1. God said that Abraham would become a great and mighty nation and that all the nations of the earth would be blessed through him. According to Genesis 18:18,19 Why did God choose Abraham?

_____

_____

2. Who taught Jacob about the power of the blessing? _____

_____

3. Give one example of God's sovereign protection or blessing taking place in the life of Abraham, Isaac, or Jacob._____

_____

4. What did Jacob do with the angel of the Lord in order to gain a blessing? He _____Him.

5. Isaac's blessing included spiritual blessings, material blessings, and divine protection. What did Isaac say to express each of these blessings? _____

_____

6. What provisions did Jacob have for his 400 mile journey to his Uncle Laban's home? _____

_____

7. When Laban blessed Jacob his flocks and possessions
   a) increased   b) decreased?
   When Laban cheated Jacob his flocks and possessions
   a) increased   b) decreased?

8. Jacob's name changed to Israel as a result of the Lord's

   _____

9. How did Jacob's son Joseph take part in blessing the world? __

   _____

   _____

10. What was the last act that Jacob performed before he died? _____

   _____

Chapter 8

HOW TO BREAK THE CURSE

"Bless them which persecute you:
bless, and curse not."

(Romans 12:14)

Suzette was as nice looking lady, 35 years of age, who had grown larger by the day until her physician told her she was dangerously over weight. He suggested a stomach by-pass to correct the problem, explaining that the procedure posed certain dangers which were probably outweighed by that of continuing to carry the excess weight. Suzette had failed in every weight-loss plan she had tried. Her lonely evenings were spent in her apartment regretting the last piece of pie she had eaten and condemning herself as she stood before the mirror. Her frustration was aggravated more by the constant failure to succeed at any effort to maintain a diet plan. Any weight loss, which would be minimal, would be followed by weight gain. She just did not know what to do until her doctor suggested corrective surgery to control her food intake for her.

I first learned about Suzette when her mother called. "Suzette has a problem with her weight that is serious, Pastor. The doctor has recommended surgery. Would you talk to her?" I was confident that Suzette could get help from God if she made an honest effort to understand the Biblical principles of blessing. When Suzette came to see me, I found that she was eager to find a solution to her problem, and I was anxious to teach her the Bible way of breaking the curse. "You are speaking curses on yourself", I told her. "You look in the mirror and tell yourself you are ugly and fat. You do not see the girl you can be in Christ Jesus your Lord. Why don't you try it God's way and see what He will do for you?" Suzette was a diligent learner, taking Scriptures to heart and speaking them over herself every day. "I apply Bible verses to myself every day just like I would take a prescribed medication", she said. She selected the weight she wanted to set as a goal for herself and blessed her self with that weight. When she looked at herself in the mirror, she told herself she was a lovely girl and that in the heart of God she was not fat.

Weeks later, I felt a tug on my coat as I stood at the entrance to our worship center. I turned to see Suzette with her hand behind her head turning in circles like a fashion model. "How do you like the way I look, Pastor?" she asked. In the next breath she exclaimed, "I have lost seventy-two pounds." I could hardly believe my eyes. It was more than I had expected. We spent a long time rejoicing over the power of God which had worked for Suzette. It was a good example of how the power of the blessing works over the curse.

The Curse of The Law

Two different types of curses are named in the New Testament, both of which greatly influence our lives. The Apostle Paul talks about the first curse in Galatians 3:10: "For as many as are of the works of the law are under the curse: for it is written, Cursed is every one that continueth not in all things which are written in the book of the law to do them." That curse upon mankind was broken in the crucifixion of Jesus Christ. "Christ hath redeemed us from the curse of the law, being made a curse for us: for it is written, Cursed is every one that hangeth on a tree:" (Galatians 3:13). Our Lord took the full impact of punishment for sin in His own body at Calvary, releasing us from the consequences of sin. "For the wages of sin is death..." Paul emphasizes in Romans 6:23a.

All informed believers rejoice in the fact that the blessing of Abraham has broken the curse of death over them. It happens each time a sinner turns to God from his sins and receives Jesus Christ into his life as Lord and Savior. At that moment, God supernaturally breaks the curse over the sinner, delivering him from the power of darkness. It is a marvelous act of God's grace granting to every repentant believer new life and freedom from the curse. Paul describes that condition as a blessing. In Romans 4:6-8, he says, "Even as David also describeth the blessedness of the man, unto whom God imputeth righteousness without works, Saying, Blessed are they whose iniquities are forgiven, and whose sins are covered. Blessed is the man to whom the Lord will not impute sin." That is the message of the New Testament. Redemption from the curse of the law is present in the blood of Jesus Christ. That blessing has been well proclaimed by the church.

The Malediction

A malediction can best be described as a curse. The power of the curse is stated both in the Old and New Testaments. Genesis 12:3 quotes God as saying, "And I will bless them that bless thee, and curse him that curseth thee..." The bitterness of the curse is described in James 3:10-11: Out of the same mouth proceedeth blessing and cursing. My brethren, these things ought not so to be. Doth a fountain send forth at the same place sweet water and bitter?" For the most part, the church has neglected the teachings in the New Testament on the way to break the power of the curse. Paul highlights the power of the blessing over the curse when he says, "Bless them which persecute you: bless, and curse not." (Romans 12:14).

Stephen, the boy mentioned in chapter 3 of this study, learned the power of the blessing over the curse. His parents began to speak blessing over his life so they could break the curse of failure over him. But something else happened which was a great source of encouragement to Stephen. He was taught how to break a curse over his own life. Stephen had misbehaved so often in the classroom that the teachers had him marked as a trouble-maker. "No matter what you do now to reform, some teachers will look on you as a failure", I told him. "You must learn the power of the words of Jesus in Luke 6:28a which say, "Bless them that curse you". I had Stephen approach my desk several times as if I was the teacher and he wanted my blessing instead of condemnation. He finally learned his part well. Then I prepared him to return to school the next day and bless his teachers who were now cursing him. Arriving at each classroom throughout the day, he approached the teacher and said, "I am very sorry for the way I have acted in your class and I ask you to forgive me. I do want to change and become a good student. You are a fine teacher. If you will help me I know I can learn in your class."

I had warned Stephen that at least one teacher would not

believe anything he said. He was prepared for her. He stood erect and listened quietly as she dressed hem down. "Who are you trying to fool", she snapped back. "You are just a troublemaker. You have caused me more trouble than anyone in all my classes. You will never make anything out of yourself. You are a failure now and you will always be one." When she had finished, Stephen replied, "I understand how you feel and I am sorry that I have caused it. But you are an excellent teacher. With your help, things will be different." the teacher's attitude changed immediately and life turned around for Stephen as he broke the curse with the blessing. From then on, he enjoyed the daily blessings of his parents over his life. His grades all changed from failure to high scores. Stephen was on his way to success.

Inheriting A Blessing

Peter said in I Peter 3:9b, "but contrariwise blessing; knowing that ye are thereunto called, that ye should inherit a blessing." Inheriting a blessing is predicated in this passage upon the willingness of the believer to give a blessing to someone else. Peter had already taught in chapter 2 that the behavior of Jesus under suffering was an example of the way His followers should react to persecution. "For even hereunto were ye called: because Christ also suffered for us, leaving, us an example, that ye should follow his steps." Peter goes on to point out that no bitterness was found in Him. He chose not to revile back when He was reviled or to threaten when He suffered. On the contrary, He is found praying for his tormenters when He suffers on the cross (Luke 23:34). Jesus was faithful to His own words in Luke 6:28 when He said, Bless them that curse you, and pray for them which despitefully use you." Every believer should follow his example as God's way for breaking the curse.

The Power of Good Over Evil

The Apostle Paul said that we were not to be "overcome of evil, but overcome evil with good." The words of Peter in I Peter 3:13 agree: And who is he that will harm you, if ye be followers of that which is good?" The fact that good is greater than evil is established. St. Augustine compared good and evil to light and darkness. Darkness is only the absence of light. So evil is the absence of good just as darkness is the absence of light. No one ever turned on the darkness. If we were in a brightly lighted room, we would not attempt to turn down the light by turning up the darkness. But we can dispel the darkness by turning up the light. In like manner, we can bring on the darkness by removing the light. Blessing is one way of turning on that light.

When we allow unjust criticism, anger and bitterness to come from our mouths, we are attempting to overcome darkness with darkness. But we never overcome evil with evil - only with good. As Hannah prayed and ministered to the Lord following the birth of Samuel, she declared: 'Talk no more so exceeding proudly; let not arrogance come out of your mouth: for the Lord is a God of knowledge, and by Him actions are weighed. (I Samuel 2:3). What comes out of our mouths makes a difference in the way we are able to overcome evil directed against us. Our actions are weighed.

When we see unacceptable behavior in our children, we can give correction to their lives without condemning them with our words. A parent can place little Johnny across the knee and spank him while speaking blessing over him at the same time. "You are a fine boy and what you have done is not acceptable. That is why you are receiving, this spanking. You are going to grow up to be a fine man. I love you and desire the best for your life." All of that can go on while the parent is correcting the child.

There is a difference between punishment and discipline. Punishment is given to inflict pain for a wrong done. Discipline is given to develop character in the child. The parent who blesses while correcting the child is administering, discipline. The parent who only punishes the child for his bad behavior, speaking condemnation over him, leaves the child under the curse of his words. "If you don't change your ways, you will probably end up just like your uncle, in jail for ten years", the insensitive parent declares. And more than likely, that is what will happen if the parent does not learn how to break the curse with the blessing.

Blessing - A Sign of Maturity

Jesus instructed His disciples saving, "Love your enemies, bless them that curse you, do good to them that hate you, and pray for them which despitefully use you, and persecute you; That ye may be the children of your father which is in heaven: for He maketh the sun to rise on the evil and on the good, and sendeth rain on the just and on the unjust." (Matthew 5:44-45). The command to love your enemy and bless those who curse you would be difficult to accept

67

if one did not understand the meaning of verse 45. "That ye may be the children of your father..." The word, 'children', in this passage is actually a word which describes a mature son - a partner with his father. A better translation would be "sons". An immature, childish Christian would have difficulty with jealousy and envy if the, sun and rain soaked the crops of his neighbor who was an unbeliever. He would complain to God that He was not fair with him. After all, I serve you and you bless that unbeliever just as much as you do me, he would protest. But the mature Christian does not judge God's love by the way He treats other people. He sees himself as a partner with God, having access to all the blessings of his Heavenly Father. His point of reference is always the Lord, not others. His desire is like that of his Heavenly Father - the redemption of his neighbor, and his enemy. As a result, he is called an "mature son" of his Father in heaven. That makes him "perfect" or "mature" just as his Father is perfect. It is from that viewpoint that the Christian is able to bless those who curse him. Paul emphasizes that point in I Corinthians 4:12b when he says, being reviled, we bless; being persecuted, we suffer it."

<u>Review – Chapter 8</u>

1. The two types of curses named in the New Testament are the curse of the _____ and the
   _____

2. Redemption from the curse of the Law is present in the _____
   _____ of Jesus.

3. A malediction can be described as a _____

_____

4. James 3:10-11 says that _____ water
   and _____ water should not come from the
   same fountain.

5. When Jesus was reviled and abused, He refused to _____
   _____ his tormentors.

6. St. Augustine said that just as darkness was the absence of light
   so _____ is the absence of _____

7. We can correct our children without _____
   them.

8. The difference between punishment and discipline is that
   punishment only inflicts _____ while
   discipline forms _____

_____

9. Blessing is a sign of _____

10. The mature Christian's point of reference is always
    the_____ and not the other people.

Answers found at end of book

Chapter 9

PLANNING A SPECIAL BLESSING SERVICE

"And it came to pass, that when Isaac was old, and his eyes were dim, so that he could not see, he called Esau his eldest son, and said unto him, My son: and he said unto him, Behold, *here am* I. And he said, Behold now, I am old, I know not the day of my death: Now therefore take, I pray thee, thy weapons, thy quiver and thy bow, and go out to the field, and take me *some* venison; And make me savory meat, such as I love, and bring *it* to me, that I may eat; that my soul may bless thee before I die."
(Genesis 27:1-4)

The air was filled with expectation as the four carefully selected couples arrived at our home for the blessing service of our sons. All of them had spent time in prayer to prepare for the occasion. They had chosen verses of Scripture for our children which they felt the Lord had shown them related to the boys' future lives. Some had written out special blessings.

My wife, Dorothy Jean, had spent all day preparing, one of the most exquisite meals of her life. She had bathed every dish with prayer asking that our guests would bring special blessings for our sons. She and I had prayed and prepared personal blessings gleaned from a study of the Bible. The desire of our hearts was to see our children experience the favor of God. The scene was set for one of the sweetest experiences our household has ever received.

Planning a special blessing service for your child will provide an unforgettable experience for every member of your family. This study will help you plan a unique, personal blessing service for each child. The child who has been prepared ahead of time to expect to receive something special from the Lord will remember the experience for years to come. But the most important outcome of the experience will be the positive results for the child. Many children have recognized the lasting effects of the blessing on their lives. They learn to expect their parents to bless them regularly.

Resources For Blessing

There are seven resources to draw from to prepare you to do the best job of blessing. Creative parents will be able to develop their own ideas, using these resources as springboards to make their own plans. Just make sure that everything you do is in agreement with the Holy Scriptures and you will have a blessed experience with your children. As one happy father wrote, "I guess it goes without saying, the message the Lord gave you (about blessing) has had a tremendous impact on our family and friends." God's plan of blessing would be a great source of encouragement to anyone who prayerfully uses it for the good of his family. Let us look at some of the resources which will help prepare you to bless your children.

The Desire of Your Heart

It was by faith that Isaac blessed Jacob and Esau and it was by faith that Jacob blessed both the sons of Joseph (Hebrews 11:20-21). They were able to see the favor of God resting upon their sons. Out of that ability to visualize the desires of their hearts for their sons, they declared their blessings.

Jesus exercised that same grace when He was blessing His disciples. Matthew 5:3-12, commonly called the Beatitudes, is a series of blessings which Jesus spoke over His disciples at the beginning of their training period. Every major experience they had is embodied in the beatitudes. They received what Jesus imparted to them through the blessings spoken in the beatitudes.

Jesus also expressed the desire of His heart when He called them the "salt of the earth" (Matthew 5:13) and "the light of the world" (Matthew 5:14). Similar desires can be identified by parents who can then speak them over their children in the form of blessings. Jesus was able to see what His disciples would become through the Word He was planting in their hearts. He knew the Holy Spirit would take that Word and bring it to maturity in the lives of His followers. Since the first teachings of Jesus were filled with blessings, we can believe that the disciples were encouraged to believe that everything Jesus said would take place in their lives.

In Luke 22:31-32, Jesus said to Peter, "Simon, Simon, behold, Satan hath desired to have you, that he may sift you as wheat: But I have prayed for thee, that thy faith fail not: and when thou art converted, strengthen thy brethren." Jesus saw beyond the temptation and subsequent failure of Peter in his denial of Jesus to the future success of Peter. He said to him, "when thou art converted". He said "when". In spite of the fact that Jesus knew that Peter would deny Him three times (V.34), Jesus saw beyond Peter's unacceptable behavior to visualize his success.

Jesus could have also told His disciples that, if they stayed with Him long enough, some day they would become the salt of the earth and the light of the world. That is what I would probably have done if I had attempted to train twelve unruly, unregenerated men like the disciples. I would have said, "I am not sure that you will ever become apostles, so you are going to have to work very hard to change." But, Jesus instilled in them the belief of what they would become even while He was teaching them the basics of their Christian life. Isaac and Jacob used the same desire of their hearts to speak blessings over their children. They spoke it by faith. What their sons were to become was already a reality in the hearts of their fathers. They used their desire as a resource to bless. With a clear vision of the potential resting in the life of the child, the blessing can be spoken with authority and confidence.

The blessing can also be given even during a time of discipline. All discipline should be given to form good character in the child, not just to punish him for a wrong committed. The discerning father can turn his son over his knee and say, as he is spanking, "you are a fine boy and that type of behavior is unacceptable. You are going to grow up to be an outstanding man." First, the father speaks a blessing; then he paddles him. That father has the ability to see beyond a temporary failure in his son's character. The son is fortunate to have a father who can bless even when he is disciplining his son. If parents do not believe in the future of their children, they will hinder their progress instead of helping. Pray that God will give you a vision of what your child is in the heart of God - then declare that over his life!

Isaac understood the importance of desire. In Genesis 27:3-4, he said, "Now therefore take, I pray thee, thy weapons, thy quiver and thy bow, and go out to the field, and take me some venison; And make me savory meat, such as I love, and bring it to me, that I may eat; that my soul may bless thee before I die. He wanted to feel good before he began to speak blessing over his son. Knowing that the words which would come out of his mouth would have great power in the life of his son, he planned to eat his favorite meal prepared by his son before he began to speak. Then, with appreciation, his words would flow with greater anointing over the life of his boy. Isaac reached that attitude through eating his favorite meal. It can also be reached through prayer, fasting and a study of the Word of God. The point is that the blessing should be spoken when the desire is the greatest.

Working through this study will help to prepare your soul before you attempt to bless. Others who want to learn how to bless their children should complete this study before beginning a regular program of blessing. Then you will have a more thorough knowledge of the principles of blessings and the reasons for blessing.

Personal Insights into Your Child's Life

Your child has natural talents and abilities which have been invested in him or her by the Lord. They were born with those abilities. The words that you speak over your children to bless the latent talents in their lives will help to bring those abilities to the surface. Many children grow up with undeveloped talents locked up inside them because the parents did not speak blessings over them as a way of encouraging the expression of the talents. The patriarchs looked carefully at their children and used the natural resources in them to help prepare the blessing to be spoken.

Special Inspiration from The Holy Spirit

The Holy Spirit gives revelation to parents when they pray and fast about the blessings to be spoken over their children. The prophetic word comes forth many times when parents sincerely seek revelation from God before speaking blessings over their children. The friends you invite to your home for a special blessing service should be encouraged to pray for wisdom and revelation about your child before they arrive. Many times they will bring words written out or beautifully printed to present to your child. The Holy Spirit will give special insight into the abilities of the child, providing the correct words to encourage the proper development of those talents.

The child may not be aware at the time of the blessing of the significance of all that is said. Yet, the blessings will have their positive effect on his life, Later in life he will look back upon the experience to confirm that what was said was indeed from the Lord. The words spoken will have become a reality in his life.

The Promises of God

You are encouraged to search the Scriptures to find the promises which speak to the life of your child. Then incorporate those Scriptures into blessings which you will speak over him on a regular basis. God will bless and enhance your words as you weave their names into the promises you speak. I have found that I can take my child's name and place it within the Scriptures in the following way, using, for instance, Psalm 1: "Blessed is (William) that walketh not in the counsel of the ungodly, nor standeth in the way of sinners, nor sitteth in the seat of the scornful. But (William's) delight is in the law of the Lord; and in His law doth he meditate day and night. And (William) shall be like a tree planted by the rivers of water, that bringeth forth his fruit in his season; (William's) leaf also shall not wither; and whatsoever (William) doeth shall prosper." In this way, the Word of God will come alive to you personally causing you to feel that it is directed to your child with more purpose than you would otherwise feel.

Peter, the recipient of so many personal blessings from the Lord, certainly understood the power of promises when he said, "Whereby are given unto us exceeding great and precious promises; that by these ye might be par-takers of the divine nature, having escaped the corruption that is in the world through lust." (2 Peter 1:4). The promises of God should be collected and prepared in a special way for the benefit of your children. Abraham "staggered not at the promise of God" (Romans 4:20a). Use the promises with great confidence when you are preparing blessings for your children.

What Other People Say About Your Child

When our children were growing up, people would sometimes comment on their good behavior when we were not with them. Knowing some of the attitudes Mother and I had to deal with in the home, I often wondered if they were talking about the same child I knew. Yet, after thinking it through, I realized that those friends were seeing the better part of our children. They had the ability to behave properly and they had done so at the right time. Now it could have been that those people had also seen some attitudes in our children which were less desirable - yet they had chosen not to tell us about those moments. I learned a lesson as I listened to my friends - that the good in my child is as important as the bad. Listening to them helped me to identify positive traits in the lives of my children. Now I could concentrate on those when I prepared a blessing service.

Do not discount the possibility of using evaluative testing to help you identify aptitudes and abilities in your child. Ask for testing results from your child's school which will help you understand your child better.

The Desires of Your Child

Listening to your child will help you begin to understand the desires of his heart. You need to know how the desires got into his heart in the first place and whether they are noble in character. The child who has been allowed to view the wrong television programs or read unhealthy material will have corrupted desires. Adjustments to your child's lifestyle will result in adjustments to the desires of his heart. One youth minister said, "When I take a group of young people away on a retreat, removing, them from television and other adverse influences, the desires of their hearts change quickly. Formerly, they desired the things of the world; now they desire the things of God."

Jesus saw desire as important to getting one's prayers answered. In Mark 11:24, He said, "Therefore I say unto you, What things soever ye desire, when ye pray, believe that ye receive them, and ye shall have them." It takes time to listen to your children and identify the desires of their hearts. But it is necessary if you are going, to use their desires to help you impart blessings to them.

On one occasion, one of my children told me about the desire he had for something in his life. I immediately said no because I did not have the personal resources to provide what he wanted. Later that day, the Lord spoke to me and said, "It does not pay to be a good boy, does it?" I was corrected in my spirit with the realization that I had turned him down only because I could not provide it myself. I went quickly to his room upon returning home and said, "Son, today the Lord has corrected me. I told you no about that request because I cannot personally provide it for you. But I want you to know that I appreciate you and the life you are living. You study hard and make good grades; you work hard and you are respectful to your mother and me. I really do want to know the desire of your heart and I want to bless that into your life." We then knelt down in his room and spent some time in prayer. Then I said, "Son, I want to bless you with the words of my agreement. Matthew 18:19 says that God honors agreement. "I bless you, son, with the desire of your heart today." Within a few weeks, he had received that which he had desired. It proved to be a wonderful blessing in his life.

The Meaning of Your Child's Name

Books are available which give the meaning of most names. But you can also give your child a Christian name. Search the Scriptures to find a Bible name which most accurately expresses the desires of your heart for your child. You can also research the meaning of your child's present name. If the name given at birth expresses the desires of your heart, use it in your blessing ceremony. If it doesn't come up to your expectations, use the new Christian name to describe his life. Then release upon your child the full meaning and impact of that name, expecting God to form those positive character traits in his life.

<u>PROGRAMING A SPECIAL BLESSING SERVICE</u>

Your special blessing service for your child should be planned ahead of time so that all those you invite will have sufficient time to prepare for the event. That should include time for them to pray and fast if they so desire to prepare their hearts to impart blessings to your child. It would be well to ask them to study this material before they come for the blessing service. They could either do it alone or you could meet weekly for several weeks to listen to the cassettes and review the study material. It is important that those you invite understand the principles of blessing before they come to the special blessing service. They should also be prepared ahead of time with a blessing for your child. These should be written out. Their attention should be directed toward the child receiving the blessing.

Now, here is a program to follow to prepare for the blessing service. First of all, you need to prepare your child. Teach your child the principles given in these eight lessons. Study the Scriptures given in the lessons together so that he will see how God has used the blessing in the Bible to bring His favor upon sons and daughters.

Have your child prepare his own blessings which he wants to speak over each member of his family and to his friends. His blessings to them should be in the form of expressions of appreciation for their influence in his life.

Encourage your child to memorize his favorite verses of Scripture to be quoted during the blessing service. He might like to select a poem which has been a favorite in his life, or a hymn or chorus which has been encouraging to his life. A friend can be asked to sing the hymn. Do everything you can to prepare your child for a very special time in his or her life.

Select your guests carefully. Make sure that they are ready so that they will not show up for the service unprepared. If they wish to bring a special gift to your child, let them do so.

Plan your meal well ahead. Prepare a special meal, including some of the favorite dishes of your child. Let the child know that this meal is for him or her in their honor. When you have completed the meal, leave the dishes to be cleaned later and move directly into the room where the blessing ceremony will take place.

When the ceremony begins, let your child begin with his Scripture and words of appreciation for each member of the family and for friends. Then the parents should follow with the blessings they have prepared to speak over him. After that, the other members of the family, brothers, sisters, and grandparents can speak their blessings. Finally, let each of the friends who have prepared a blessing read it to him.

A Blessing to Model

It would be inappropriate to end this study without giving a suggested model one can use for blessing children. I am going to be bold here and use a blessing my wife prepared for each of our Sons before their special blessing service. The model used here was given to our younger son but the words were similar for both except for the difference in the meaning of their names.

"To my beloved son, John Wesley Ligon. Your name means 'The Beloved of God' (Luke 1:15-17, John 1:6-7). 'There was a man sent from God whose name was John. The same came for a witness, to bear witness of the Light that all men through him might believe.'" She went on to talk about how Scripture had meaning in his life. She referred to his name, John, and the meaning of that name. She pointed out to him that he was named after the founder of the Methodist Church, John Wesley. She talked about the life and character of John the Baptist and John Wesley.

Then she moved into the blessing saying, "To my son of my womb and covenant before God and man, surely you fragrance, my son, is like the fragrance of a field which the Lord has blessed. Therefore, may God give to you the dew of heaven, of the fatness of the earth, and plenty of grain and oil. Do not give your strength to women nor your ways to that which destroys covenant men. It is not good for men to drink wine and intoxicating drink lest they drink and forget the law and pervert the justice of all who are appointed to die. Open your mouth. Judge righteously and plead the cause of the poor and needy. Open your mouth and preach that Gospel in the wisdom, knowledge and power of God. May you and your household always love God with all your heart. Fear Him and reverence His Name, for out of the heart proceed the issues of life. May God bless you with a virtuous, God-fearing, wife who is beautiful in spirit, soul and body. May she be a person with a servant heart, a teacher in the love and admonition of the Lord, imparting special grace to your children. May she extend her hand to the poor and needy and may the law of kindness, gentleness and generosity be expressed from her heart. May your wife be blessed as Rachael and Leah, the builders of the household of faith and be like a fruitful vine in the heart of your home. May your children be as olive plants in the house of the Lord and as pillars sculptured in palace style and polished with the Spirit and Glory of God. May the names of you and your family be written in the Lamb's Book of Life and may you be found with faith and faithfulness when the Lord comes. May the zeal, the love and power of God always be evident in your life.

"I bless you with good health and may God's angel go before you and cause you to succeed. I say blessed are you because you have made Jesus Christ your Lord and God. I love you dearly and bless you with my life, love and prayers."   -Mother

Well, there is the blessing of a mother spoken over her son who is so precious to her. It was spoken over each of her sons in a special service for them. It was prepared after much meditation, prayer and fasting. It was expected to be fulfilled, even if he were to go through a difficult time during which it appeared that he was going to do just the opposite.

When you have worked through all the resources given in this chapter, and you have begun your blessing ceremony, you can expect the prophetic Word of God to be expressed over your child.

Then the anointing of the Holy Spirit will come upon him and he will receive blessing from God.

I pray that these teachings will bless you and your child greatly.

<u>Review – Chapter 9</u>

1. Isaac understood that the blessing was to come forth from deep within his _____ (Genesis 27:1-4)

2. The child should be prepared ahead of time, before a blessing service to expect to receive something special from the _____ _____

3. When Jesus blessed His disciples in Matthew 5, He was able to see _____ before they occurred.

4. Jesus always told His disciples you _____, not one day you will _____

5. Knowing your child's _____ abilities will help you prepare to bless.

6. Special inspiration to bless will often come when the parent is _____ or _____

7. Pray for _____ and _____ before you bless your child.

8. The resources available to help prepare a blessing are (7) - ___

   _____

   _____

   _____

   _____

   _____

   _____

   _____

9. Through God's promises, we partake of the_____ _____ nature.

10. A special _____ service should be planned for each child.

Answers found at end of book

Chapter 1

1. Children; 2. Children; 3. Failing to impart the blessing to them; 4. Bless; 5. The hearts of the fathers and children would be turned back to each other; 6. The blessing; 7. Redemption, Imparting Divine favor; 8. Because the spoken blessing imparted God's favor; 9. He blessed the people; 10. Bless

Chapter 2

1. Through the blessing God spoke over man; 2. The spoken blessing; 3. Blessed, Receives tithes; 4. They blessed her; 5. Irrevocable; 6. The Angel of the Lord; 7. The High Priestly blessing; 8. Unregenerated; 9. Bless them; 10. Bless

Chapter 3

1. The Priestly blessing; 2. By speaking the blessing; 3. God; 4. The spoken word; 5. By confessing with the mouth Jesus as Lord; 6. Hearing the Word of God; 7. Covenant; 8. Blessing; 9. The blessing of Abraham; 10. Recognition that children are a gift of God through whom covenant is expressed

Chapter 4

1. They were included in the Faith Hall of Fame in Hebrews 11; 2. Isaac; 3. Covenant plan; 4. Isaac; 5. When they were very small; 6. Failing to consider the Word of the Lord when blessing; 7. Older should serve the younger; 8. Rebekah; 9. Genesis 48; 10. Numbers 6:24-26

Chapter 5

1. Redemptive; 2. Right; 3. Ephraim; 4. Right; 5. By blessing his sons; 6. Jesus Christ; 7. The Life of Jesus, Jesus receives Calvary; 8. Redemptive; 9. Preference; 10. Rachael and Leah

Chapter 6

1. Sweet; 2. Visualize; 3. Potential; 4. Faith; 5. Discipline; 6. Verbal; 7. Verbally; 8. Hands; 9. Expect; 10. Irrevocable

Chapter 7

1. That he may command his children and his household after him to keep the way of the Lord by doing righteousness and justice, so that the Lord may bring upon Abraham what He has spoken about him; 2. His father Isaac and grandfather Abraham; 3. 4. Wrestled him; 5. May the Lord grant you the A) Dew of Heaven, B) The fatness of the earth and plenty of grain and wine, C) Cursed be everyone that curseth the and blessed be everyone that blesseth thee; 6. The clothes on his back, the staff in his hand, and the blessing of the Lord; 7. Increase, Decrease; 8. Blessing; 9. He prophesied a seven year worldwide famine and was given the wisdom and authority to administer the answer; 10. He blessed his son's

Chapter 8

1. Law and the malediction; 2. Blood; 3. Curse; 4. Sweet, Bitter; 5. Curse; 6. Evil is the absence of good; 7. Condemning; 8. Punishment inflicts pain while discipline forms character; 9. Maturity; 10. The Lord

Chapter 9

1. Soul; 2. Lord; 3. Blessings; 4. Are, Become; 5. Natural; 6. Fasting, Praying; 7. Wisdom and Revelation; 8. Desire of your heart, Personal insight, Special inspiration, The promises of God, What others say, Desires of your child, Your child's name; 9. Divine; 10. Blessing

Additional Resources can be found online at:
www.thefathersblessing.com using the store link or you may call
us direct at **912-267-9140**

Recommended materials and Study Guide

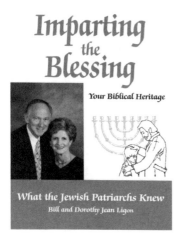

Imparting *the* Blessing

Your Biblical Heritage

What the Jewish Patriarchs Knew
Bill and Dorothy Jean Ligon

Blessing   Audio 4 CD's $30.00

Recorded at a live seminar. Pastor Ligon, his wife DJ, and son William, Jr. unfold the Godly gift of verbal blessing. Learn what the bible says about releasing the favor of God on you and your family. You will see that God reveals His heart to bless His people. Understand the redemptive power of the blessing. Learn to defend against the verbal curse. Hear how to plan a productive blessing service.

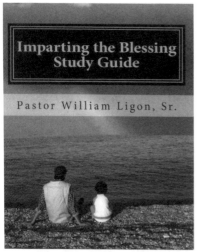

Imparting the Blessing
Study Guide

Pastor William Ligon, Sr.

Blessing Study Program $55.00

This 12 session guide provides our most effective program for study groups to learn the verbal blessing. DVD lessons used in conjunction with the study guide provide the platform to learn and practice the verbal blessing. Abraham, Isaac, and Jacob understood the power of this blessing. They imparted it to their children! Moses and Aaron obeyed the Lord's command to bless. Peter, Paul, and the Lord Jesus all effectively verbalized blessing. Don't miss using this teaching in your bible study group. Order today.

Extra books are can be ordered for class members. $12.00

The Anointing
$20.00 4 CD Album

The bible speaks of two anointings, one that fades and one that abides. Learn about the anointing that abides so that you too can develop an abiding relationship with the Holy Spirit.

Steps to Maturity
$20.00 4 CD Album

This series compliments the blessing materials. The bible indicates four stages of spiritual growth that move a person from childhood to maturity in Christ. Learn how to be brought to spiritual vision and responsibility. Become a father in the faith.

Leadership Series
$20.00 4 CD Album

Pastor Ligon teaches in this series the attitudes necessary to bring forth mature Christian leaders. Great insight for developing good leadership traits in children, adults, and leaders in the Church.

Also Hear
"Faith Foundations"
$20.00 4 CD Album

89

Building up Your Faith	Single CD	6.00
Resurrection Life	Single CD	6.00
God's Blessing For Your Health	Single CD	6.00
Covenant Blessings	Single CD	6.00
Breaking the Generational Curse	Single CD	6.00
The Power of Obedience	Single CD	6.00
The Way of Restoration	Single CD	6.00
Pleading the Blood of Jesus	Single CD	6.00
The Father's Faith	Single CD	6.00
Children the Church of Tomorrow	Single CD	6.00
The Blessing It Really Works - Grant Cole Testimony	Single CD	6.00
Beholding His Glory	Single CD	6.00
A Call To Excellence	Single CD	6.00
Grant Her Honor	Single CD	6.00
Christ The Perfect Man	Single CD	6.00
Christ In You	Single CD	6.00
Faith Foundations	4 CD Album	20.00

The Children's 10 Commandments Project

11 books teaching the 10 Commandments; reveal God's will for building Christian character.

8th Commandment Book

Bobby Bear loves a fresh baked honey pie. Who can resist! He finds one that belongs to Benny Bee and soon learns the 8th Commandment, thou shall not steal.

4th Commandment Book

One Sunday in Sunny Valley beavers are busy chewing down the neighborhood. How will they learn about the 4th Commandment, honoring the Sabbath? What happens in this wonderful story leaves everyone smiling!

7th Commandment Book

June and Skippy are two happy bunnies that fall in love at church. They practice God's great wisdom and keep their love alive. They keep the 7th Commandment. Yea! It's very sweet.

9th Commandment Book

It's a birthday party and a train story all wrapped up into one great adventure. Bobby Bear learns to tell the truth. See how it happens and how the quick thinking of Will and Wyatt (train engineers) saves the day.

10 Commandments CD

The author weaves a wonderful story for each Commandment. This is a great way to follow God's admonition to teach His Commandments to your children. Enjoy all 10 stories as the author tells these tales.

Phone Orders: (912) 267-9140

Web Orders:

www.thefathersblessing.com - then use

The "Store" link

Imparting the Blessing
Study Guide

Pastor William Ligon, Sr.

Consider leading a small group in a study program on the blessing. Invite your friends and neighbors to join you one night a week to watch a DVD instructional by Pastor Ligon and discussed the weekly lesson from the study guide.

The feedback from study groups has been phenomenal! Begin your study group today.

SO WHAT DO I DO NOW?

SO WHAT DO I DO NOW?

Dallas Groten

BETHANY HOUSE PUBLISHERS
MINNEAPOLIS, MINNESOTA 55438
A Division of Bethany Fellowship, Inc.

Copyright © 1989
Dallas Groten
All Rights Reserved

Published by Bethany House Publishers
A Division of Bethany Fellowship, Inc.
6820 Auto Club Road, Minneapolis, Minnesota 55438

Printed in the United States of America

Library of Congress Cataloging-in-Publication Data

Groten, Dallas, 1951–
    So what do I do now?

    Summary: Gives advice to young people on handling difficult moral and ethical problems from a Christian point of view.
    1. Teenagers—Conduct of life. 2. Teen-agers—Religious life.
[1. Conduct of life. 2. Christian life] I. Title.
BJ1661.G76   1989   241   89–14
ISBN 1-55661-033-5

I dedicate this book to my godson Jason Dallas Peterson, and to all children everywhere who have cried tears they cannot understand. With this book I declare war on the cause of those tears.

I also dedicate this book to the one who has loved me despite my imperfections—my wife, Caroline.

DALLAS GROTEN is a counselor for a public school. He lives in southeastern Minnesota with his wife, Caroline, and two children. He is author of three other books.

Contents

1. If He Wants to Marry Me?...................... 15
2. When I Want Revenge?......................... 19
3. When She Expects Me to Break a Promise? 22
4. If I'm Too Embarrassed to Show My Face? 26
5. If I Suffer for No Reason? 30
6. If She's Ugly?................................. 33
7. If They're Devil Worshipers?..................... 36
8. If She Wants to Go to Bed With Me?.............. 40
9. If I Want to Be a Marine? 46
10. If My Right to Have Fun Hurts Someone Else?...... 51
11. If He Says We're All the Same? 54
12. When I Know It's Wrong but I Still
    Want to Do It? 58
13. If I'm Tired of Saying "No"?...................... 61
14. If I Get Pregnant? 64
15. If I Don't Graduate? 68
16. If I'm in Love? 71
17. When I Can't Be What My Father
    Wants Me to Be?............................... 74
18. If I Don't Want to Be a Super-Christian? 78
19. If I Want to See Her Naked? 82
20. If My Teacher Says There Is No Right
    or Wrong?..................................... 85
21. If I Told a Lie? (Even If It's
    Only a White One)............................. 89
22. If He Won't Let Me Be My True Self? 92
23. If My Family Wants Me to Make a Lot of Money?.... 95
24. When My Brother Tells Me He's Gay?.............. 98
25. If I Don't Like Myself?........................ 103

8

26. If My Best Friend Wants Nothing to Do With Me? ... 106
27. If I'm Ashamed of My Father? 109
28. When I Know He's Selling Drugs in School? 112
29. If I Can't Be Kind to Him? 115
30. If He Tells Me He Wants to Kill Himself? 119
31. When I Want to Change the Past? 123
32. When I Don't Want Life to Be the Way It Is? 127
33. If I Can't Take It Anymore? 131
34. If My Religion's Driving Me Crazy? 134

Introduction

If I Could Hear God Talk, What Would He Say?

*G*od, I'm in trouble. . . !"

"I don't know what to do. . . . So what *should* I do now. . . ?"

Silence.

"Tell me something, God. Tell me something that will help me with my problem. . . !"

Silence.

"I think you're there, Lord, so I'm going to listen. You don't need to talk to me in some booming voice like in those old Charlton Heston movies. *Just speak to me in any voice.* I need your advice so bad, God, that my insides are all torn up. *Please* speak to me. . . !"

Silence . . .

"I'm listening. . . !"

9

Silence . . .

Silence. Have you ever turned to God in desperation, needing to know the answer to a crucial question of right and wrong? Did you wish God would tell you audibly in plain English exactly what to do? And you soon found the only thing such wishing brings is silence?

God does not speak to most of us in an audible, plain-English, Charlton-Heston-movie-voice most of the time, but the silence does not mean He does not speak. In fact, God is talking to us constantly, we just don't know how to listen.

This book demonstrates that God *does* talk to us. He talks to us through His Word.

The Bible claims to be the written Word of God (2 Tim. 3:16). We need to study God's Word, but Bible study is never meant to be undertaken in a sloppy, haphazard fashion. We also need good teachers and the support of a church that honors the Word. We must not look at the Bible only as a book we can use to solve our personal problems, despite their complexity, by merely gleaning proof texts.

No, the Bible is not a book of magic amulets. We can't take chunks out of the Bible and ignore the rest. It is important to understand that since the very beginning of Christianity, the Church, despite intensive Bible study, has not yet arrived at a unified agreement on several doctrines (baptism, the importance of the Lord's Supper, predestination, etc.). And the Bible does not claim to give specific guidance on all issues for all Christians living in every age.

We need to see how God talks to us through His written Word as we prayerfully grow in Him and follow Him as our Lord and Savior. For after all, we are not ultimately saved by obeying the principles of the Bible, but rather by God's grace and through faith in the Christ of the Bible. We are called to worship the God of the Bible, not the Bible of our God.

Keeping this in mind, understand that in this book you will meet young men and women who confront very complex, real problems. Each person is forced to make a decision—in some cases, agonizing decisions over what is right and what is wrong. In every situation, the young man or woman comes to the same point of frustration, wanting to shout: "SO WHAT DO I DO NOW?"

The "God's Voice" sections of this book do not pretend to be the absolute, audible voice of God. Instead, "God's Voice" is composed of relevant Bible passages that are helpful to the young man or woman of each chapter in making a responsible decision in relationship to his or her problem. "God's Voice" usually contains more than one Bible verse, because God's answers tend to be multifaceted. Therefore you can use this book in the following ways:

1. To read key Scripture passages that must be known in making specific decisions involving right and wrong. Such passages can become foundations within you for present and future ethical decision making.

2. To help you in your decision making. The problems the characters confront are problems familiar to many young people. Therefore the Scripture passages can help you see how the Bible addresses specific problems where a decision must be made. Each chapter title identifies the problem.

3. To show you specific sections of the Bible that address vital subjects so that you may further read such passages in context and in depth.

4. To help you see that God definitely states that certain things are right and certain things are wrong. Therefore a person cannot make a responsible, moral decision without looking to God's Word.

5. To help you see the wisdom and practicality of the Bible so that you will be encouraged to prayerfully read God's Word while seeking out good Bible teachers within a Christian church.

6. To help you understand the character of God.

7. To help you understand that God does indeed talk to you through His written Word.

In short, "God's Voice" is a general description of what the Bible says about certain moral issues through specific, representative Scripture passages, to help you in your struggle with ethical decision making. For greater effectiveness, it is suggested you read each chapter chronologically.

The questions at the end of each chapter will help you creatively wrestle with contemporary problems so you will be better prepared to make sound moral decisions. But the questions are also for family and group discussion, so that you can benefit from the insight of other minds.

You will find that the young men and women in this book have very difficult decisions to make. However, I never tell you what their final decision is. In fact, it is safe to assume that some of the young people decided not to make any decision at all, but instead ran away from their problems.

We often find ourselves in conflicts that don't allow "comfortable" solutions. And yes, God's Word does give strong guidance, but even the right moral choices bring pain and sacrifice and can only be successfully carried out with the help of God. If we do make the wrong choice, despite the tragic consequences, God's Word clearly informs us that if we sincerely turn to God for mercy, He, because of His Son Jesus Christ, will forgive us completely.

No. This is not a book of easy answers. It is a book of hard questions. A book that encourages you to seek the hard answers found only in the gracious hands of the Living God.

Chapter 1

WHAT DO I DO

If He Wants to Marry Me?

No!... Impossible.... Mara thought, as she looked out over the audience that crowded the gymnasium. He had come after all—and there he sat, in the sixth row of folding chairs, smiling at her.

She smiled back.

She'd thought she'd never see him again—not after the last time.

It was a sticky June evening, and he was wearing an army uniform. His face tormented and crushed her. Yet the thought that he'd come so far to see her graduate filled her with joy and a strange, painful comfort.

... He really must care, she thought.

Principal Calhoun cleared his throat and leaned close to

15

the podium so that his mouth almost touched the microphone. "It is my honor and privilege," he said, "to introduce you to a young woman we expect to do great things—our valedictorian, Mara Blake. . . ."

She rose and walked to the front of the platform in the thunder of applause. In a haze, she recited the speech she had carefully plastered to the walls of her brain. And all the while her mind was besieged by thoughts of the guy in the army uniform who sat before her. Visions attacked her mind: the time she was sick, lying in a hospital bed; Todd had refused to leave her side. He was always so encouraging.

Who knows—? the thought passed quickly through her head, *maybe he's the reason I'm even standing on this platform now. . . .*

Later that evening, in the front seat of his father's car, his hands were all over her. Mara broke away from him and crossed her arms. It was then that Todd reached into his pocket and pulled out a tiny box. He opened it and took her hand, gently placing a small diamond ring upon her finger.

"*Todd?*" she cried in astonishment. She didn't expect this—didn't *want* this.

"I want you to marry me," he said. "I love you."

"I thought we were through. I've made plans."

"Don't argue," he insisted gently.

"But you're going to be stationed overseas. And you know I've been accepted at . . ."

"I'm taking you with me. They have colleges in Germany, too, don't they? Besides, I'm sick of always saying goodbye."

As Todd wrapped his arms around her, pulling her close to him, Mara could feel the hammering of her heart. She knew that the next words she spoke would change her life forever.

What should Mara Blake do?

Other Voices:

"You can't let a gorgeous guy like him get away from you. He's perfect. Sure he's asking you at the wrong time. But there's no such thing as a right time for love. You're not going to find many guys like him in the world."

"You're too young. You've got those scholarships and your dreams of being a lawyer and all. If he really loves you, he can wait at least until you are able to start a career."

"Can't you do *both*? Sure, you'll lose that scholarship if you go to Germany. But *someday* you'll be able to go on to school, even though you're married."

"Marriage isn't all that it's cracked up to be. It's plain hard work. Especially when you start having kids."

"Do you *love* him? It seems to me that's the main question. And don't you think every woman should be married? This may be your only chance."

God's Voice:

At a major crossroads, like this one, is exactly the time when you need to spend time alone with the Lord. The advice and "helpful" thoughts of other people will never take the place of prayer or listening to God. He *may* speak to you through others—but He will definitely guide you by filling your heart with peace and conviction.

As Solomon wrote,

Trust in the Lord with all your heart
and lean not on your own understanding;
in all your ways acknowledge him,
and he will make your paths straight.
                    (Proverbs 3:5–6, NIV)

And Jesus Himself promised,

My sheep *will* hear my voice. . . . (John 10:27, KJV, emphasis added)

Your Voice:

1. Do you feel Mara loves Todd?
2. Are her fears about possibly losing "the one and only guy for her" realistic?
3. What are the advantages of Mara and Todd getting married? The disadvantages?
4. What do you think would happen if she married Todd?
5. Should they get married now?
6. What's right about modern marriage? What's wrong?

Chapter 2

WHAT DO I DO

When I Want Revenge?

Several weeks before, Stephen had slouched on the sofa in the cluttered living room, opening and closing the blade of his jackknife. The blade had felt cold. Though he had rented a video, he had paid almost no attention to the television screen.

Marcini's face would not leave his mind. Their hatred for each other had been building up since middle school. Almost daily, Marcini ridiculed Stephen: He called him "wimp," "ugly," "gay"; once he had cornered Stephen and, with six guys watching, slapped him around until his mouth started bleeding.

Last week in the locker room after phy ed, Marcini bragged about his date with Angie, the girl Stephen secretly worshiped. He described her as if she were a piece of meat. The guys roared.

Stephen detested him.

Two days later, Stephen heard that three guys were going to wait outside Marcini's house this Saturday night to jump him when he came home from the basketball game. One of the guys, Charlie, had been expelled from school for knife-fighting. For some odd reason he had always been friendly with Stephen. Maybe it was because both of them lived in the government housing projects, and neither one had an "old man" around. Or maybe it was just because they both hated Marcini, who flashed around his money and loved to impress everyone with the Trans Am his father had bought him when he got his license.

When Charlie had noticed Stephen was listening to their plan, he looked at him. "You wanna come? We're just gonna mess up his pretty face a little."

Stephen had nodded. . . .

On Saturday night, Charlie pulled his car over to the curb one block from the Marcini's. They piled out and quietly closed the doors. Stephen felt his heart begin to race with terror. This was wrong—not just wrong but stupid. Yet all he could do was follow Charlie and the other two guys as they snuck up the sidewalk toward the large white house.

Marcini would be home any minute. He'd park his flashy car by the curb. They'd all jump him from behind. . . .

It was then Charlie pulled out the club. By the streetlight, Stephen could see the sick smile. "I'm gonna mess up his face bad. So he'll never forget what he done to me."

Stephen's hands went cold.

Did he really want to go through with this?

Other Voices:

"Nobody else has punished him for everything he's done to you. He'll just get away with it, unless you help beat up on him. You have to even it up."

"This is no good. You're gonna wind up in juvenile court. Get out of here. Fast."

"Charlie'll kill you if you back out now. It's too late."

"But you hate him. Get him. If you don't beat him up now, you're gonna wish you had for the rest of your life."

God's Voice:

If any harm follows, then you shall give life for life, eye for eye, tooth for tooth, hand for hand, foot for foot, burn for burn, wound for wound, stripe for stripe. (Exodus 21:23–24)

People have used this passage from the Old Testament as justification to seek revenge. But balance this view against other passages:

Beloved, never avenge yourselves, but leave it to the wrath of God; for it is written, "Vengeance is mine, I will repay, says the Lord." No, "if your enemy is hungry feed him, if he is thirsty, give him drink; for by doing so you will heap burning coals upon his head." Do not be overcome by evil, but overcome evil with good. (Romans 12:19–21)

Your Voice

1. What would Jesus do if he were Stephen?
2. What would Charlie do if Stephen backed out and told him why?
3. Why does the Bible say it's unwise to seek vengeance?
4. How could Stephen channel his hatred for Marcini in a positive direction?
5. What do you think will happen in this situation?
6. How can God and His grace help us to forgive?

Chapter 3

WHAT DO I DO

When She Expects Me to Break a Promise?

*M*arcy was shocked.

Her best friend, Kris, really did it. She casually walked up to her father, while he was sitting outside in a lawn chair.

"Hey Dad. . . ?" she began, innocently.

He folded his newspaper. "What is it?"

"Could you please buy a case of beer, and a fifth of Seagrams? Oh, and maybe a little vodka?"

Her father's face showed neither anger nor surprise. "Just what are you going to do with all that booze?"

"Some of my friends need it, for the party."

"Party?"

"I *told* you about it. The party at Jill Rennselaer's house tonight. Her mom's going to be upstairs while we party in the basement."

He nodded. "So if the party's B.Y.O.B., and I buy the booze and the place gets raided, Jill's mother takes the heat, and not me. *Right?*"

"Correct," Kris said, with a triumphant smile.

Her father let a resigned hiss of air slip through his teeth, "You get the money from your friends, and I'll get the booze," he said. "But you make really sure none of them drive you home. Understand?"

Out in the driveway, Kris turned the key in the ignition. "This is fantastic, Marcy!" she cried, backing out of the driveway. "When I was in the lunchline, I overheard Wilson and Mike and Sara Jeels griping that they couldn't find a buyer to get them some stuff for Jill's party. So I said my dad would do it. They almost kissed me!"

Wilson, Mike, and Sara Jeels were three of the most popular kids in school. Marcy could understand Kris's joy over her sudden acceptance. But Marcy was silent as she stared out the window.

"Kris," she said at last, "you *promised*."

"Promised what?"

Marcy turned and glared at her. "You and I both made a pledge never to get drunk. Remember?"

"Who said anything about getting drunk?"

"C'mon. A *case* of beer? Whiskey and vodka? For four people? How much are *you* going to drink—just a *sip*?"

"What's it to you?"

"You *promised* not to."

Kris rolled her eyes. "You're the only one who takes promises so seriously. Besides, we were just dumb kids. You really ought to grow up."

"And we promised to report parties like that to the police."

"Give me a break!" Kris said in disgust. She gripped the steering wheel tight. "So I suppose you're gonna turn us in. . . ?"

Silence.

"Kris," Marcy said at last, "I don't want to sound like some goodie-goodie, but what your dad's doing is wrong. Illegal. Buying stuff for minors. Suppose something serious . . ."

Kris suddenly stomped on the brake and turned the car over to the side of the road. "*You* can get out and walk!"

Marcy was startled. Then angry.

"Maybe I will," she said. Undoing her seat belt, she opened the door and got out.

"If we get raided," Kris said, her voice shaking, "I'll tell everybody *you* called the cops. You'll be trash at school."

Marcy fought to hold back the tears now. "Kris . . . I'm sorry . . . but you're my friend."

"And if you get my dad in trouble," Kris interrupted, "I'll kill you!"

What should Marcy do?

Other Voices:

"After the way Kris treated you, Marcy, you *should* report that party to the police. It'd serve her right. Even if she is your best friend."

"Look, if you call the police it's gonna ruin your life. *Everybody* will hate your guts. Jill's mother will get arrested. Wilson will get kicked off the swimming team. . . . Keep your mouth shut."

"You haven't changed. You're just like you were when you were a kid—a little tattletale."

"What if someone drives home drunk—and gets killed? If the party gets raided, it may save some lives."

"A promise is a promise."

God's Voice:

And be not drunk with wine, wherein is excess. . . .
(Ephesians 5:18, KJV)

The Bible tells us to uphold godly laws of society (Titus 3:1).

But what about a friend who is breaking the law?

As for those who are guilty and persist in sin, rebuke and admonish them in the presence of all, so that the rest may be warned and stand in wholesome awe and fear. (1 Timothy 5:20, Amplified)

Timothy 2:25 says:

He [the servant of the Lord] must correct his opponents with courtesy and gentleness in the hope God may grant that they will repent and come to know the truth. (Amplified)

Even though friendship is important (Proverbs 17:17), God tells us to serve Him only. Human friendships cannot come before our commitment to God and His laws.

It helps to know that the God who *accepts* us because of Jesus can help us make responsible decisions through the Holy Spirit.

Let us therefore come boldly unto the throne of Grace, that we may obtain mercy, and find Grace to help in time of need. (Hebrews 4:16, KJV)

Your Voice:

1. What would you do if you were Marcy?
2. What should Marcy do if she decides to do nothing—and is later plagued by guilt?
3. Suppose everyone gets drunk at the party but the police don't raid (because Marcy doesn't inform them), no one is hurt in an accident because of drunken driving, and Kris becomes good friends with Wilson, Mike, and Sara. How should Marcy act toward Kris?
4. What do you think of Marcy? Do you like her? Is she "too good"?

Chapter 4

WHAT DO I DO

If I'm Too Embarrassed to Show My Face?

*T*oday, Wayne just knew he would shine.

Just like the champions on the football and the basketball teams; like the guys with the cars that everyone wanted to drive.

Today, Wayne would be the center of attention. Yes, it would only last for a few minutes, but it would still be attention.

The bell rang, and all the kids burst out of class. In a few minutes everyone at Paramount High had packed out the auditorium. Eventually, the lights dimmed, the curtains opened, and the Annual Student Talent Show began.

At last, Wayne walked from the wings toward center stage. It was a long walk to that microphone. And his eyes penetrated into the darkness of the near-silent auditorium, seeing not a single face, yet knowing all eyes were on him.

In his mind he knew he could be a star.

The opening piano chords seeped out. Wayne announced, "Please rise for the singing of our national anthem." The pianist paused. He attacked the first line. . . .

Oh, say can you see, by the dawn's early light . . .

Sure it wasn't the type of song kids naturally go wild over. But it was the kind of song that let him show off his singing ability. He was a vocal gymnast. His voice could start low and climb. Building in power, he could carry them with him to the peak of the song, leaving them awestruck. . . .

And the rockets red glare, the bombs bursting in air . . .

Giggles. Across the huge audience, the chuckling spread like ripples.

Wayne fought to keep his voice from breaking. His face felt hot. *What are they giggling about?*

Someone shouted, "His zipper's down!"

Mid-note, Wayne looked down. *It was true!* The piano pounded along relentlessly.

In desperation, Wayne spun away from the audience, zipped up his fly, then faced them again, hardly missing a beat. Now the whole audience burst out laughing—deafening, cruel laughter.

Wayne couldn't take it another minute. While the pianist continued to stroke keys, he turned and ran off the stage.

The next day in school, everyone smirked at him. He was even given a new nickname: "The Fly." He was branded as the guy who sang in front of the entire school with his zipper down.

As the days rolled on, Wayne realized he could not shake his reputation. So he decided to transfer to a different school across town.

His father was furious. "Sounds to me like you're running away from your problems, not *facing* them."

"You don't know how hard it is," Wayne shot back. "It's hell on earth."

What should Wayne do?

Other Voices:

"Lighten up, would you? It's not the end of the world. Laugh it off. Don't transfer."

"You'll never live it down. The only way these kids'll be able to forget 'The Fly' is to forget you. Transfer."

"Here they call you 'The Fly.' There they'll call you something else just as embarrassing. You might as well tough it out here."

"In another school you'll really have the chance to be what you want to be. You won't have to live according to some image that others have molded you into."

God's Voice:

When you are tempted to run away from unpleasant situations, the Bible says the best person to run to is the God of the Bible.

David wrote:

How I love you, Lord! You are my defender. The Lord is my protector; he is my strong fortress. My God is my protection and with him I am safe. He protects me like a shield; he defends me and keeps me safe. I call to the Lord, and he saves me and keeps me safe. I call to the Lord, and he saves me from my enemies. Praise the Lord! (Psalm 18:1–3, GNB)

Your Voice:

1. Should Wayne stay at his high school or "flee" to the other school across town? Is transferring to another school the right thing to do?

2. If Wayne decides to stay at Paramount, what could he do to erase his reputation as "The Fly"?
3. How can God help Wayne in this situation? How can Wayne run to God?
4. Can you remember a situation you wanted to run from, but couldn't? How did you deal with things?

Chapter 5

WHAT DO I DO

If I Suffer for No Reason?

She had just dropped into her seat in seventh-period geometry class, when she saw the words written on her desk in red ink:

Talia Carson is a whore.

Talia felt something deep inside of her crumble. Her heart hammered. She felt all the blood rush from her face as she fought back tears.

She slid her books over the words—but still they screamed out at her.

What about the other kids who had shuffled into the room? Had they seen the words? What about Mr. Schmidt, her geometry teacher, had he read these words too? *I'll just die,* she thought.

When Talia was certain she was not being watched, she licked her index finger, moved the books, and tried to wash the ugly words off. But the letters stubbornly glared up at her. Finally, she colored over the words with a black pen.

How many kids have sat in this desk today? she worried. *Who in this school thinks that I sleep around? Or is it just that someone hates me?*

She glanced at Scott in the far row. He was studiously working on a problem, looking innocent.

I went out with him last week, she thought. *He wouldn't write something like that. Or would he?*

Her eyes moved to Beth. *Maybe she wrote it,* Talia thought. *She would. She's so proud of being a virgin. But it's easy for her—she's so ugly no guy would touch her. And she has always hated me. . . .*

The bell rang.

I can't go out in those halls, Talia thought in a panic.

All the other kids stood up, clutched their books, and headed out the door.

Mr. Schmidt cast her an inquisitive eye as he gathered up the papers.

She still sat at her desk. *I don't sleep around. I don't!*

What should Talia do? How do you fight a lie?

Other Voices:

"Find out who wrote it and make his or her life miserable."

"Listen, your friends won't believe the words. Your enemies will. There's nothing you can do about it."

"Don't go out with any guy for the rest of the year."

"There's nothing you can do about it. Just make the most of a bad situation."

God's Voice:

The psalmist wrote:

Deadly enemies surround me; they have no pity and

speak proudly. They are around me now, wherever I
turn, watching for a chance to pull me down. They are
like lions, waiting for me, wanting to tear me to pieces.
Come, Lord! Oppose my enemies and defeat them!
(Psalm 17:9b–13, GNB)

This is the prayer of an innocent person. Psalms like this
one are good to read in a situation like this.

Jesus had some awful things said about Him. He responded
with, "Father, forgive them; for they know not what they do,"
(Luke 23:34).

Your Voice:

1. Why do the innocent suffer mistreatment from others?
2. Is Talia over-responding to this situation?
3. What positive things can Talia do about her pain?
4. What would you do if you were Talia Carson?
5. In what ways can God help Talia?
6. Is it good to pray for the defeat of your enemies?
7. How did Christ handle insults?

Chapter 6

WHAT DO I DO

If She's Ugly?

Scott did not go out on blind dates. Period.

But one night, in a weak moment, he said yes. His best friend, Mitch, had a cousin named Rob, whom Scott didn't know very well. But he understood that Rob was handsome and was always talking about girls. When Rob offered to set Scott up with a pretty girl from another school, Scott decided to give him a try. It would be a double-date, and Rob would drive.

On the night of the date, however, Rob called and said that he'd come down with the flu. But he talked Scott into taking Vicki, the blind date, to the basketball game anyway, sight unseen, because she looked "fantastic."

Scott stumbled into the bright lights of Vicki's living room as her mother held the door open for him. He waited on the couch for Vicki to come downstairs.

Then he saw her. *No!*

Vicki was anything but fantastic-looking. How could she be the same girl Rob had bragged about? Her hair looked like it had been through a food processor. Her nose sprawled across her face like a bath mat. And that mole on her neck—it had to be the size of a nickel. And where did she pick up all those extra pounds? *Fat city.* Or so he thought.

But at least her clothes were attractive, Scott tried to console himself, but it wasn't working very well.

At the game, they had only sat in the bleachers half a quarter when Scott told Vicki he had to go to the men's room. He got there and hid in a stall.

I can't let anyone see me here with someone as ugly as Vicki, he thought. *If they do, I won't have any chance of taking out other girls. They'll think I'm scraping bottom. The guys'll rip me apart. I know what they'll say—"What are you doing with that hog?"*

Then Scott thought of his car, parked outside. All he would have to do would be to slip out of the men's room, sneak out into the lobby, through the front door, and drive home.

But what about Vicki? Do I just leave her? he argued with himself.

She doesn't go to this school. She doesn't know anybody. He knew she'd look for him, wait for him. When he didn't come back, she'd probably call home and ask her father to come and get her. Maybe she'd be crying.

This ugly girl in the attractive clothes . . .

What should Scott do?

Other Voices:

"You can't just *leave* her there."

"You've got your reputation to work on, buddy. You need all the help you can get. If too many people see you with such an ugly girl, you'll never have a chance to take out the pretty girls in your school. You'll be labeled a nerd forever."

"If you ditch her, she'll tell. Even if she doesn't know anybody in your school she'll still tell somebody that you were her date and you ditched her. And that would get around, too."

"You won't take her out again. Leave early before too many people see you. You'll *never* see her again anyway."

God's Voice:

The Bible let's us know that inner beauty is much more valuable than outer beauty.

Charm can be deceptive and beauty doesn't last, but a woman who fears and reverences God shall be greatly praised. Praise her for the many fine things she does. These good deeds of hers shall bring her honor and recognition from even the leaders of the nations. (Proverbs 31:30, TLB)

Your Voice:

1. The above Bible passage gives one reason to believe true beauty consists of what a person does, not in what they look like. What do you think about this?
2. Who is the more beautiful person in this story?
3. Does inner beauty manifest itself in outer beauty?
4. How can you make yourself more beautiful on the inside?
5. How can Christ make you beautiful?
6. Do you think Scott went back into the game, or did he dump Vicki?

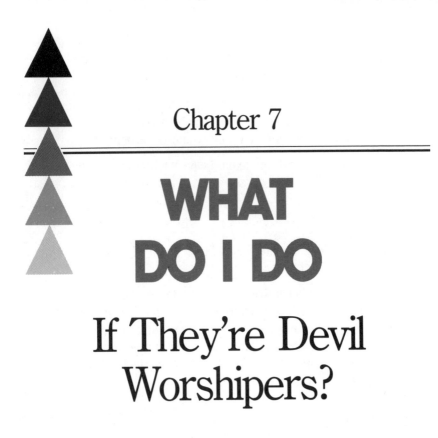

Chapter 7

WHAT DO I DO

If They're Devil Worshipers?

*A*s they stood in the lunch line together, Larry somehow knew what Tricia was going to say even before she opened her mouth.

"They're devil worshipers."

Larry just laughed. *"Tricia*, don't be such a geek. *Devil worshipers?* C'mon. It's only a party. I'm gonna go."

Tricia was insistent. "I know they're pretty quiet, but I also know they meet at night in the underground tunnel at the state park. And they call themselves *The Coven*. They listen to weird music."

"So what," Larry replied, reaching for a plastic tray and some silverware. "Maybe they think you're weird. Who said you were the judge, anyway?"

"Have you heard the stuff they listen to? *Gross!*"

"No," Larry admitted. "But I've been hanging out with some of them a little bit. They're okay. They don't *talk* about people," he said pointedly. "And they're smart, too," he went on. "They call themselves *spiritual adventurers*, not devil worshipers. They say they're building themselves up—you know, really loving themselves by seeking power through stuff like astral projection and channeling and talking to wise spirits. A lot of good people do stuff like that. Even my counselor at Bible camp. You wouldn't call him a *devil worshiper*, would you?"

"I don't know," Tricia faltered. In a moment, she said, "But Chad Ferris belongs to *The Coven* doesn't he?"

"I guess so. I don't know him at all."

"Well, he told me he hated Christ. And I've heard rumors about all kinds of gross things they do. Animal sacrifices. Blood drinking. Drugs. They even have a hit list. Kids in this school are on it. They do voodoo curses on each kid on the list."

"Right!" Larry snorted. "Well . . . It's a free country. The guys in *The Coven* have a right to do what they want. Why does it bother you, anyway? And maybe *The Coven's* some sort of religion that helps people love and believe in themselves, I don't know. Isn't that what Mr. Thompson's always trying to tell us in health class? Believe in yourself? Who are you to put them down?"

As the two left the lunch line carrying their trays of food, Tricia pleaded. "Don't go to their meeting tonight at the state park, Larry. *Please. . . ?*"

Now Larry felt uneasy and strange inside.

What should he do?

Other Voices:

"Look, you don't know what goes on there. The bad stuff you heard is probably all rumors. At least go and check things out."

"But some of the covers on the tapes they listen to in school have pictures of dead babies and broken crosses. . . ."

"They're just rebellious. All young people are rebellious. Didn't your old man listen to the Rolling Stone's record *Sympathy for the Devil* when he was a kid? The Beatles and even Elvis were considered agents of the devil in the old days. . . ."

God's Voice:

He [Manasseh] . . . practiced divination and magic and consulted fortunetellers and mediums. He sinned greatly against the Lord and stirred up his anger. (2 Chronicles 33:6)

But when you follow your own wrong inclinations, your lives will produce these evil results: impure thoughts, eagerness for lustful pleasure, idolatry, spiritism (that is, encouraging the activity of demons) . . . and there will be wrong doctrine, envy, murder, drunkenness, wild parties, and all that sort of thing. Let me tell you again as I have before, that anyone living that sort of life will not inherit the kingdom of God. (Galatians 5:19–21, TLB)

The Spirit says clearly that some people will abandon the faith in later times; they will obey lying spirits and follow the teachings of demons. Such teachings are spread by deceitful liars, whose consciences are dead, as if burnt with a hot iron. (1 Timothy 4:1–2, GNB)

Don't let your people practice divination or look for omens or use spells and charms, and don't let them consult the spirits of the dead. (Deuteronomy 18:10–11, GNB)

Keep all your magic spells and charms. . . . You are powerless in spite of the advice you get. Let your astrologers come forward and save you . . . They will be like bits of straw. . . . (Isaiah 47:12–15, GNB)

Your Voice:

1. Do you think the group that meets in the state park is a bunch of devil worshipers?
2. Do you believe in a personal devil?
3. There exists in North America a Satanic Church. Do you think this "church" should be protected by the Constitution, just like any other religion?
4. Where do you draw the line in popular music between "this song is all right to listen to" and "this song is wrong to listen to"?
5. Do you think satanists tell potential new members, "Come and join our group. We're satanists"? Or are they more subtle in their recruitment?
6. Should Larry go to the group's meeting in the state park?
7. How can we separate rumors from reality?
8. Can you be a Christian and do the spiritual exercises Larry said his Bible camp counselor participates in?
9. What do you think of ouija boards? Tarot cards? Seances?
10. If something is "spiritual" is it automatically blessed by God?
11. How important is the Christian Church to you?
12. How much have you explored the excitement and power of prayer? How can you do this?
13. What should our attitude be toward any group that denies the Lordship of Jesus Christ and participates in spiritual exercises the Bible calls evil?

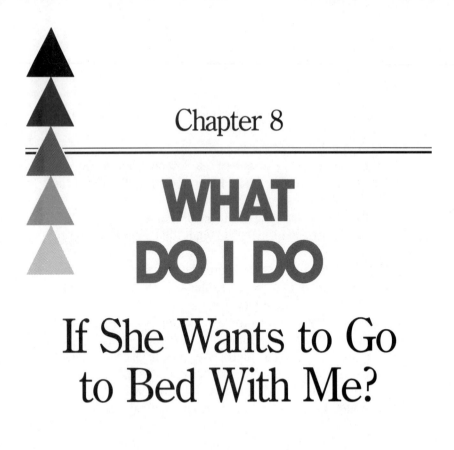

Chapter 8

WHAT DO I DO

If She Wants to Go to Bed With Me?

*I*t was prom night.

The small movie theater was packed tight with people. Mark thought he was going to suffocate. He told Lucy he would be right back and then left her munching popcorn. He elbowed his way through the crowd of unfamiliar faces in the lobby and pushed open the double doors. The welcome breezes of the warm spring night splashed his face as he stepped out into the darkness.

Dodging cars, he walked swiftly across the street and staggered into the park. He leaned against a large oak tree, wrapped his arms around the trunk, and hung his head.

Mark didn't know how long he stood there hugging the tree. Suddenly, he started. Somebody was standing next to him.

"You drunk?"

The voice was familiar. It sounded like his big brother.

Mark turned to look at the figure. "Justin?" he said. "It *is* you. No. I'm not drunk—just . . . I don't know, I got real nervous—or something. What are you doing here?"

"Just out taking a walk," Justin replied. "Why aren't you trying to get Lucy into the back seat of a car instead of in the park hugging a tree?"

Mark sat down on the grass and, for a moment, said nothing. Justin sat next to him. Finally, Mark said, "You won't believe it, but that's the problem. Lucy wants to go to bed with me."

"What's wrong with that. . . ?" Justin laughed.

"I don't know what to *do*. Lucy's been around. Lookin' at magazines is one thing. But . . ." His voice trailed off. "I can't do it."

"Just tell her you don't want to," Justin shrugged.

"I already said a lot of stuff to her," Mark replied. "I've been workin' on this for weeks. Tonight she told me about a college guy who wants to take her to this cabin on a lake. How'm I supposed to compete with that? I knew I'd lose her when she went to college."

Justin pulled a familiar plastic packet from his pocket. He'd obviously been to the drug store. "Do you need one of these?"

"No. Just forget it."

"You're scared. Like I said, tell her you don't want to. She'll understand."

"She *won't* understand. She says she still loves me. But things haven't been exactly good between us since she went away to school. She says sex might make things better. But I think it'd be wrong. . . ."

There was silence, except for the singing of crickets.

"I'd better get back to the movie," Mark said at last.

What should he do?

Other Voices:

"But she'll say, if you don't do it, it means you don't love her."

"A person who loves you doesn't push you into doing things you don't feel right about doing."

"Most girls do it and like it."

"Studies show that lots of girls don't do it."

"Go for it. It'll prove you're a man."

"What proves that you are a man is deciding what you believe is right and sticking to your beliefs."

"Lose your virginity. Get it over with."

"If you're even *considering* this, you must not respect your body. Besides, she's been away at college for a year. You don't know whom she's been messing with."

God's Voice:

The Bible never ducks the issue of sex. If you need convincing, read *The Song of Solomon*. God created sex—for both procreation and pleasure (Genesis 1–4). Since He's the Creator, then we should know and follow His guidelines.

The Bible is clear when it says that sex is at its best when it's between a man and a woman who are faithfully married to each other.

Marriage is to be honored by all, and husbands and wives must be faithful to each other. God will judge those who are immoral and those who commit adultery (Hebrews 13:4, GNB).

This does not mean marriage is perfect, or that dehumanization and sexual degradation do not exist within certain marriages, or Paul would not have needed to admonish marriage partners to love each other (Ephesians 5).

But the marriage state is so precious in God's sight that it is compared to Christ's love for the church. Therefore, He says,

> Shun immorality. Every other sin which a man commits is outside the body; but the immoral man sins against his own body. Do you not know that your body is a temple of the Holy Spirit within you, which you have from God? You are not your own; you were bought with a price. So glorify God with your body. (1 Corinthians 6:16–20)

What about pre-marital sexual practices other than sexual intercourse—such as sexual touching or mutual masturbation or oral sex? Some people say, "It's not intercourse, so it's not *really* sex."

Yet it's easy to see the dishonesty in this statement. But the question many young people agonize over today is, "How far can we go before it is sin?" The list of questions you will find at the end of this chapter may help in evaluating the world's pressures to conform, the urges of our own bodies, and God's will for us in this matter.

Recently, government agencies have had to issue statements about "safe sex" procedures to avoid AIDS and other sexually transmitted diseases. They have gone so far as to warn people to "have sex only with one mutually-faithful, uninfected partner." God is wise, so He suggested that a long time ago!

Yes, sex is a powerful force—but it's a force that can lead to unwanted pregnancies, abortion, or fatal disease if we let it run out of control. "Safe sex" is not an option the Bible offers to the unmarried person.

Yet, if you have sinned in this area, you need to know that God will forgive:

> If we confess our sins, he is faithful and just and will forgive our sins and purify us from all unrighteousness. (1 John 1:9, NIV)

Whether or not you have already experienced sex, the wise person today lives his/her life in line with God's Word, by His help and grace. If it's important to concentrate on following Christ, then abstaining from sex before marriage is a precious gift to God. This seems harsh to the modern mind, but Scripture affirms that God is worth even the most difficult of sacrifices.

> I appeal to you therefore, brethren, by the mercies of God, to present your bodies as a living sacrifice, holy and acceptable to God, which is your spiritual worship. (Romans 12:1)

Your Voice:

1. What is God's "will" for your sex-life?
2. What is adultery? Fornication? Check a Bible with a concordance.
3. If the risks of pregnancy and disease are lessened through birth control devices and condoms, does this make it okay to engage in sex outside of marriage?
4. Many young people complain that the people who preach about waiting until marriage are those adults who are married. This makes it easier for them to preach, but they don't understand the temptations today's young people face. What do you think about this?
5. Do you think sexual intercourse is as great as everybody says it is?
6. Just when does a marriage relationship begin?
7. Do people ever seek in their lovers character qualities that are only found in God?
8. How can a friendship with Christ help you become a mature sexual being?
9. How can you glorify God with your body?
10. What would you do if you were Mark?
11. How likely are you to meet the person you will marry while you're still a teenager?
12. You may truly care about someone, but there is always the possibility that you will break up with that someone. How intimate can you be without feeling embarrassed and awk-

ward if you are no longer going together?
13. What's good about kissing and hugging? What's bad?
14. If you were to marry today, would you feel embarrassed about your past?
15. How does the Holy Spirit use our feelings of guilt and uncomfortableness to get our attention?
16. The saying goes: "If you really love each other, you will wait for marriage." How then do you draw the line that will keep you within God's law?

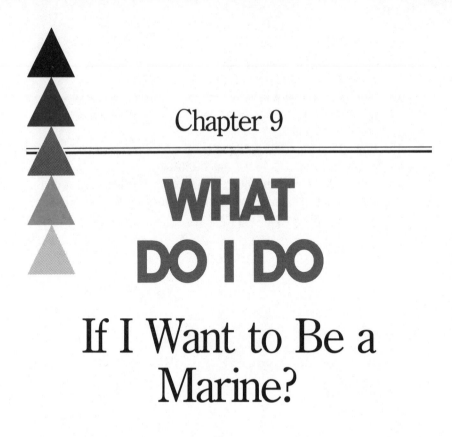

Chapter 9

WHAT DO I DO

If I Want to Be a Marine?

*J*ust when she thought she finally had her life together, her church went and messed things up.

After a long, inner struggle that went on throughout all of her junior year and most of her senior year, Colleen Williams was ready to enlist in the Marines.

She had received high scores on the Armed Services Vocational Aptitude Battery. Her recruiter used many forceful words to try to convince her that enlisting was a godly thing to do. "This country," he said, "needs to be defended from outlaws and war mongers who want to destroy it. If you love God and love your country, joining the military is right, and not wrong." That had clinched it—finally!

Then Mr. Simons, an elder in the church, came along. He

had heard that Colleen was about to enlist. He'd heard that she'd wrestled with her decision for a long time, and had finally decided, within her own conscience, that joining the Marines was *not* in violation of her faith.

He spoke to her one night in her living room:

"Colleen," Mr. Simons said, "You know we're a peace church. We don't believe in our people joining the military. You know this, don't you?"

"Yes Mr. Simons, I do."

"So why are you going to sign up?"

"Because I think it's a smart thing to do. I don't see it as a sin."

"Colleen, the military may be all right—for others."

"But I feel good about it," she interrupted. "I want to join more than anything right now."

"But can you be a peacemaker, as the Bible tells you to, if you are carrying a gun? How can you 'turn the other cheek'? Can you honestly see Jesus as a soldier?"

Colleen hated this. She could feel the confusion coming back. With more anger than she intended, she replied, "The Marines aren't going to disappear if I don't join them. Would the world be more peaceful if there were no armies? I mean, the terrorists would have a ball. If we have a military in this country, shouldn't it be full of Christians who love peace, so that some war-loving creep of a dictator will think twice before starting a war? Besides, chances are I'll never be anywhere near a war."

Mr. Simons shook his head, gravely. "But Colleen, you're a leader in the church. The other young people look up to you. I'm afraid that if you join, other young men and women from our church will join, too. But it won't be because they have hammered this matter out in their consciences as you say you have. They'd only join to emulate you. You may unconsciously be leading our young people to act against their own consciences."

"I'm still going to join, Mr. Simons," Colleen said, even though she felt shaken inside.

"I think you're making a terrible mistake." He continued to shake his head.

What should Colleen do?

Other Voices:

"Jesus said, 'Blessed are the peacemakers,' and 'Turn the other cheek.' Peace is a fruit of the Spirit. How can you be a Christian and in the military at the same time?"

"In the Old Testament, God told armies to go and make war with other nations. In the book of *Revelation*, Jesus leads a cavalry of warriors. Certainly it's okay to be a Marine."

"When Peter cut off that soldier's ear, Jesus was mad. Real mad. He rebuked Peter and healed the soldier."

"It's a Christian's duty to defend his country against godless communism."

"But war is not godly. It's mutilating babies and raping and killing people who are enemies now, but five years later could be our friends."

"We sing 'Onward Christian Soldiers' in church don't we? Besides, if we have a strong enough military, then we won't have wars. A Christian *can* be in the service and still be a Christian."

God's Voice:

Government has a God-given task to protect the good and to restrain the evil by force of law in order to prevent the destructive anarchy that comes from human disobedience to God's love:

> Everyone must obey state authorities, because no authority exists without God's permission, and the existing authorities have been put there by God. (Romans 13:1, GNB)

Abraham was a powerful instrument in God's hand, but we read in Genesis 14:13–15 that he fought in a battle. David was a warrior (1 Samuel 17 and 30). Several times in the Old Testament, God promised His people victory in battle (Leviticus 26:7–8). And we read of Israel's numerous military victories (Joshua 10:1–27 is just one example).

Paul compares the Christian to a soldier:

Take your share of suffering as a good soldier of Christ Jesus. (2 Timothy 2:3)

He goes on to state:

No soldier in service gets entangled in civilian pursuits, since his aim is to satisfy the one who enlisted him. (2:4)

Paul seems to be taking it for granted that the military is necessary in an imperfect and fallen world.

But Jesus has some strong words in favor of nonviolence:

You have heard that it was said, "An eye for an eye and a tooth for a tooth." But I say to you, Do not resist one who is evil. But if anyone strikes you on the right cheek, turn to him the other also . . . You have heard it was said, "You shall love your neighbor and hate your enemy." But I say to you, Love your enemies and pray for those who persecute you. (Matthew 5:38–44)

Leo Tolstoy, Mahatma Gandhi and Dr. Martin Luther King, Jr., were inspired by these passages to develop their philosophies of nonviolent and passive resistance. There are Church historians who remind us that the early Christian Church's disciplinary measures disapproved of believers serving in the army. And some people will tell you contemporary Christians must be nonviolent and responsible pacifists.

Blessed are the peacemakers, for they shall be called the sons of God. (Matthew 5:9)

Your Voice:

1. Is the Bible confusing in its statements on the military, war, and violence?
2. Can a Christian serve in the military? Or even fight in a war? Must the Christian only serve in non-combat positions?
3. Can a Christian be a pacifist?
4. Can we really live by Jesus' words? What about policemen? A teacher under violent, physical, and verbal attack from a student? A soldier who must defend his or her country from terrorists who want to destroy the innocent? What about a president or prime minister who sees an enemy attacking his or her nation?
5. In the past, the Christian Church formulated a "Just War" theory, stating that under certain conditions, a war may be justly fought. Can a nuclear war ever be a just war?
6. Should a Christian living in the Soviet Union be a Soviet soldier?
7. What would you do if your country became involved in a war you considered unjust?
8. Should a Christian watch violent movies or television shows?
9. How can we show love to our enemies? Can a soldier in combat against an enemy love that enemy?
10. What would you do if you were Colleen?

Chapter 10

WHAT DO I DO

If My Right to Have Fun Hurts Someone Else?

*H*e was tall and rangy.

The three young men, each mounted on an all-terrain vehicle, watched him stride toward them out of the woods. His face was red and pinched with anger. But there was also something about him that made the man look harmless.

"What're you guys doing?" he demanded.

The three friends looked at one another and started smirking. Willis, the biggest one of the trio, shot back, "What's it *look* like we're doing?"

"Looks like you're going to drive those vehicles down the stream," the tall man said.

"Well, aren't you *smart?*" Willis said, sarcastically. Stan, his friend, started laughing. But Bane, his younger brother,

51

began to feel a little ashamed of the way Willis was mocking the man. All he wanted to do was start up his four-wheeler and get away from the geek.

"You kids have no right to do that," the tall man said, the anger in his eyes still blazing.

"You don't own the woods," Willis challenged, "Ferguson does. He lets *anybody* in this woods. And we asked permission too."

"If you drive down that stream you'll tear up the banks and destroy the ecological balance, ruining it for trout fishermen."

Bane wished that Willis would start his engine and tear out of here. What was the sense of starting an argument with some hiker? But Willis went on. "Look," he said, "we came a long ways to ride these things. Ferguson said we could ride in his woods, so we have just as much right to be here as you or some trout fisherman."

The tall man stepped toward Bane. "You've got to *earn* the right to see the beautiful sights in a woods," he said. "You guys are destroying the quiet and the beauty by riding on those things. You run over wildflowers, knock down saplings, and scare away the deer. Those things are obnoxious. . . ."

"Shut up!" Willis shouted. Suddenly he started up his engine, turned the four-wheeler around, and spun dirt at the man with his rear wheels. The tall hiker jumped to get out of his way. Stan nearly fell over laughing.

But Bane felt a stab of guilt. All he could do was stare into the impassioned face of the strange man.

What should he do?

Other Voices:

"You've got to think of yourself. Have some fun."

"Sure it'd be fun to tear down stream. But don't do it. Sometimes you've got to sacrifice for the common good."

"You're machine is made for woods like this. Go for it."

"You can ride that thing anywhere. But the trout fishermen can only fish in streams."

God's Voice:

I can do anything I want to if Christ has not said no, but some of these things aren't good for me. Even if I'm allowed to do them, I'll refuse to. (1 Corinthians 6:12, TLB)

Your Voice:

1. Who is right, the hiker or the three young men?
2. What are some ways we can be caretakers of God's natural creation?
3. What would you do if you were Bane?
4. What are some lawful things to do, which we probably shouldn't do?

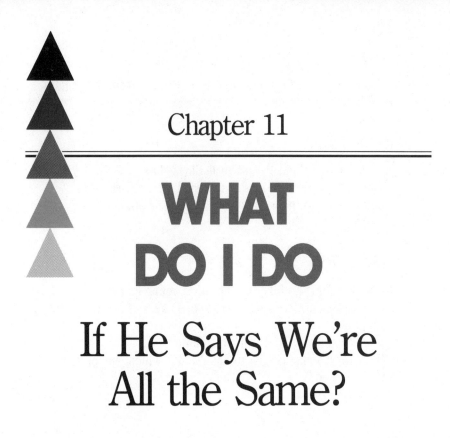

Chapter 11

WHAT DO I DO

If He Says We're All the Same?

Suzi was dusting old man Leonard's living room when she saw him glance out the front window. Suddenly he swore, and hurried to the front door.

Bic, Mr. Leonard's German shepherd, thrust its head through the crack, growling and baring its sharp teeth.

"*Sic 'em, boy,*" Leonard rasped. "*Sic 'em!*"

The dog blasted out the door, barking savagely now. Suzi ran to the front window and watched as the dog bounded across the front yard, snarling at the lean, young man with long blond hair, who turned his startled face toward the dog. Now the dog was in the air, lunging. . . .

Two feet from the young man's head, the dog crashed against the wire fence that stood between them. Furiously, the dog drilled its snarling muzzle through the chain links. The young man reeled back a little on the sidewalk.

Suzi looked questioningly at Mr. Leonard.

"Just wanted to show him," the old man muttered. "Down at the barber shop they say the kid's a queer. I just want him to know he ain't welcome in this town!"

Queer? Suzi thought. *Just because he has long hair?* She knew the guy who had now hurried off down the street. Sure he had long hair—but he wasn't gay.

"C'mon Bic!" Mr. Leonard called out, and the dog trotted back into the house. The old man closed the door, turned and faced Suzi with a grin. "Just scared him a little bit. Didn't do him no harm."

Suzi continued dusting the table as Mr. Leonard shuffled through the living room. "Don't want no queers living in this neighborhood," he said. "Don't want him drinking from the coffee cups at the diner. Or using public toilets." Then he let out a heavy grunt as he dropped down on the sagging, old couch.

But Suzi was angry. She dropped the dust rag. "You can't get diseases that way," she said, trying to control her voice. "You can get them even if you're straight. Besides, I know him. He's straight. You can't judge a guy just because he has long hair."

At first the old man looked stunned. Then his lip curled in anger. "I'm paying you to clean my house," he growled, "not to shoot your mouth off."

Suzi felt color rushing into her cheeks.

"You kids are all the same," Mr. Leonard rambled on. "Don't know the meaning of hard work. Disrespectful. And all you think about is sex and drugs. That's it. But God is fixing you with this AIDS business, that's for sure!"

For a moment he paused. Then he looked at her belligerently. "You gonna dust that table or look at it?"

With glaring eyes, Suzi turned back to the table, dusting it in fury.

All the same? Suzi thought. *He says blacks are all alike and Jews are all the same too. . . .*

"Where'd you learn that stuff you were spouting off?" he asked, interrupting her thoughts.

"Health class," she responded coldly.

Then he proceeded to verbally blast public education, while she grew more angry.

I'd quit working for the old jerk, she fumed inside. *But I need this job. . . .*

"I pay good money for taxes. . . ." the old man raved.

. . . I'll quit, she shouted inside *. . . But I need the money. . . .*

What should Suzi do?

Other Voices:

"How can you work for a guy who would turn his dog on an innocent man? The bigot! Quit!"

"You need the job. It's not hard work. The hours are good. Just hate the guy—but shut up, don't say anything."

"Tell him what you think. If he fires you, at least you told him off. If he doesn't fire you, at least you can work for him with a clear conscience."

God's Voice:

God is a master artist. He made each of us to be unique individuals.

Even everyone that is called by my name: for I have created him for my glory, I have formed him, yea, I have made him. (Isaiah 43:7, KJV)

Be tolerant with one another and forgive one another whenever any of you has a complaint against someone else. You must forgive one another just as the Lord has forgiven you. And to all these qualities add love, which binds all things together in perfect unity. The peace that Christ gives is to guide you in the decisions you make; for it is to this peace that God has called you together in one body. (Colossians 3:12–15, GNB)

Your Voice:

1. Should Suzi be tolerant of Mr. Leonard's views?
2. Why is saying that all young people, all blacks, or all women are the same faulty thinking?
3. What is bigotry? How can you combat it?
4. How do people develop the views Mr. Leonard holds? Do you know someone like him?
5. How can Suzi creatively share God's love with Mr. Leonard?
6. Should she quit her job?

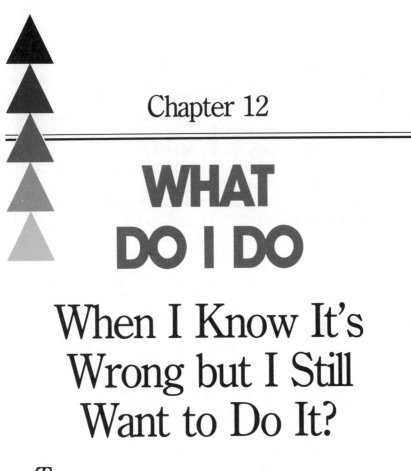

Chapter 12

WHAT DO I DO

When I Know It's Wrong but I Still Want to Do It?

*T*he tobacco tasted good.

The first time Jason tried a wad of smokeless, he swallowed more juice than he spit out. He was sick for a whole day. But after a few tries, his chewing improved. Now the taste of smokeless tobacco between his lower lip and his teeth was something he enjoyed. It gave him a feeling that he was "big time."

One afternoon, Jason gripped the clippers and proceeded to trim the tops of the hedges in the backyard. He knew his father had watched him push the pinch of tobacco into his mouth. But he wasn't worried. His father had seen him sneak a chew before. Why should he say anything now?

"Jason."

"Yeah?"

"What've you got in your mouth?"

"Nothing," Jason said casually, and continued to snip away at the tops of the hedges.

"You're lying," his father said in anger. "You're chewing tobacco, aren't you?"

No answer.

"*Aren't you?*"

"Yes, I am," he said, finally.

His father let a hiss of air escape between his teeth. "I suppose you think that smokeless stuff is pretty safe. Right? Well I was just reading an article in the paper. . . ."

And the article said chewing was no good, Jason thought. *I know that. I know it's no good for me. I even remember from parochial school how the teachers taught us that all kinds of stuff is bad for you.*

"I don't want you chewing that stuff," his father concluded. "So spit it out."

"But I like it. . . ."

"I said, *spit it out!*"

Jason spit the plug of tobacco out of his mouth so that it arched high over the hedge and out of view.

"Now," his father said, "You're going to give up that filthy habit—right?"

Jason nodded, but he was thinking, *soon as you're out of sight I'm going to have another chew. . . .*

"I want an answer," his father demanded.

"Sure, Dad," Jason lied. "I'll give it up."

What should Jason do?

Other Voices:

"Even if you enjoy it, the stuff is bad for you. It can hurt your body."

"Those Church-school teachers thought they were God. *They* aren't perfect. Neither is your dad."

"If something's wrong, and you do it anyway, you've got to pay the price and face the consequences of your wrong actions."

"Is it *really* wrong? If you enjoy it, do it. Everybody's got a little vice they indulge in."

God's Voice:

Young people, enjoy your youth. Be happy while you still are young. Do what you want to do, and follow your heart's desire. But remember that God is going to judge you for whatever you do. Don't let anything worry you or cause you pain. You aren't going to be young for very long. So remember your Creator while you are still young, before those dismal days and years when you will say, "I don't enjoy life." (Ecclesiastes 11:9—12:1, GNB).

Your Voice:

1. Does the previous Bible verse give you permission to do whatever you want?
2. Why does it seem God is against so many activities people appear to enjoy? Is God a killjoy?
3. If you are not specifically told in the words of the Bible whether a practice is right or wrong, how can you *tell* if it's right or wrong?
4. Health experts have warned that nicotine is a dangerous, addictive drug and that tobacco causes cancers of various kinds. But is there anything wrong with the *moderate use* of it?
5. We can know something is wrong and then go ahead and do it anyway. How can we bring this tendency within us under control?

Chapter 13

WHAT DO I DO

If I'm Tired of Saying "No"?

*T*im?"

"Yeah?"

"I'm skipping school tomorrow." JeriAnne confided.

"What're you gonna do?"

"I'm goin' over to Amy Lawrence's house."

"Amy's? But she and the rest of 'em are having a party."

"I know," said JeriAnne matter-of-factly.

"But they all get blitzed. Not just drinking. They use 'coke.' "

"I know."

"Then why are you going to her house?"

"Because of Paula, I guess."

"Paula?"

"Yeah. A year ago she was a lot like me—good student,

pretty straight and all that—but unpopular. Then, she started going to Amy's parties. They all accepted her after that. She became a part of the group, if you know what I mean."

"But why do you want to be a part of 'the group'?" Tim pressed.

"Because they've got all the hunks after them. Sounds like a good group to be in to me. And they *finally* asked me to one of their parties. So I'm going."

"But JeriAnne, don't be a jerk. Don't you see they invited you because you're the president of the Just Say "No" Club? They think it'd be a riot to get you blitzed."

"Don't worry," she said defensively, "I'll just drink enough to show 'em I'm not strange or anything."

"But what about all the kids in the club who look up to you? They elected you president. You may influence them to say 'yes.' "

"I don't influence anybody."

"You *do*. It may not seem that way to you. But you do."

"Yeah, but where has saying 'no' gotten me? Saying 'no' never made me popular. Saying 'no' never made the hunks chase after me. I'm sick of saying 'no.' It's too hard."

"Don't do it," Tim persisted.

"My mind's made up," said JeriAnne. But inside she began to feel like a hypocrite.

Other Voices:

"Everybody wants to be popular. I can't blame you."

"But if you have to destroy your whole personal value system to be popular, then it's not worth it."

It's hard being called strange or a geek and all that because you're different from everybody. Go for it. Go to the party."

"You don't know how many kids look up to you. You have no idea how popular you really are. Just because kids don't come up to you and say they admire you for saying 'no' doesn't mean they don't admire you."

God's Voice:

So let us not become tired of doing good; for if we do not give up, the time will come when we will reap the harvest. (Galatians 6:9, GNB)

But when we do become tired of doing good, God has promised to help us:

Fear not, for I am with you, be not dismayed, for I am your God; I will strengthen you, I will help you, I will uphold you with my victorious right hand. (Isaiah 41:10)

God is our strength and a very present help in trouble. (Psalm 46:1)

Your Voice:

1. How do you feel the members of the Just Say "No" Club would respond if JeriAnne were to get drunk or experiment with drugs?
2. What responsibilities do we have to younger people who may look up to us?
3. What positive benefits will JeriAnne reap both now and in the future by staying clean?
4. What is more important than just saying "no" in matters of right and wrong?
5. What are you willing to give up to be a part of "the group"?

Chapter 14

WHAT DO I DO

If I Get Pregnant?

*T*he bedroom door was closed. Mara Blake lay on her bed thinking, *I'm going crazy.*

First her boyfriend, Todd, had gone back to Germany. Then, she missed her period. So she waited, counting the days, for one week—two weeks—three. But a month passed. And now she knew.

As Mara lay on her bed now, she pictured the stern faces of her mother and father. She saw herself facing them. "Mom, Dad—I'm pregnant." Then their faces shattered in her mind's eye, as she dissolved in tears.

She sobbed and sobbed. And now she felt as though the fear was choking her. A thousand ugly thoughts attacked her mind. *I didn't want it to be this way. No!*

The next day, Mara drove herself to the clinic. How she wished she would hear those calm and reassuring words from the doctor: "The test was negative."

But words of the young doctor who examined her were so final, so cold, so definite: "You are about five weeks along, I'd say."

"How?" she asked bitterly. "I'd just started on the pill! Did I use it wrong?"

Later, back in her room, Mara's friend Dani, a college student, sat beside her.

"What about your parents?" Dani asked.

"I haven't told them yet."

"You *haven't?*"

"No way. Dad had that heart attack last year. And my mother. . . ."

"Does Todd know?"

"No. Oh, Dani—he just asked me to marry him. If he finds out, he'll come back here and use this to force me to marry him. I don't even know if I *love* him anymore. I want to get married someday—and maybe even to Todd. But not *now*. Not just because I'm pregnant. I wish I were dead."

"You understand what you have to do, don't you?" Dani asked. "I can help you."

Mara shook her head. "I know what you're going to say. But I don't think I'm ready for *that* either."

"Mara, I don't want to pressure you. I know it's a gross and terrible thing, but it's legal. It just seems like it's something you have to do. It's safe. . . ."

"But Dani. . . ."

"What's your alternative?—bring the baby to term? How are you going to keep *that* from Todd?"

"But I want to keep the baby."

"Mara—think! You've got all those scholarships, and you're accepted at a great college. You want to be a lawyer, remember? Having a baby will wreck all those years of hard work. You've got to think of your*self* and your future."

"But the *baby*. . . ?"

"It's not a baby yet. It's a fetus. Just tissue. Get an abortion."

Mara blew out a sad breath so that it caused a lock of her hair to puff upward. "Maybe I'll miscarry," she said.

"Fat chance," Dani said.

What should Mara do?

Other Voices:

"If you get an abortion you'd be a murderer!"

"It *is* the lesser of two evils. You don't want to be forced into a marriage you're not ready for. Even if you carried your baby to term, your parents would be heartbroken. Better to end this pregnancy before they even find out."

"Have the baby and give it up for adoption. It's not fair to deny life to an innocent little baby just because you couldn't control yourself."

"It'll be easier giving up the fetus now than it will be giving up a newborn baby you've carried inside you for nine months."

"We're talking human life here, not a piece of tissue. *Human Life.*"

God's Voice:

The Bible contains no verses that speak directly about abortion, but there are many passages that speak very clearly about the sacredness and value of all human life. David wrote about God's activity in human life from before birth:

> For you did form my inward parts, thou didst knit me together in my mother's womb. I praise you, for I am fearfully and wonderfully made! (Psalm 139:13–14)

> Thus says the Lord who made you, *who formed you from the womb* and will help you. . . . (Isaiah 44:2)

> Before I formed you in the womb I knew you, and before

you were born I consecrated you. (Jeremiah 1:5)

See also Job 10:9–11.

Perhaps the most dramatic indication of life within the womb is when Mary was pregnant with Jesus and she visited Elizabeth who was pregnant with John the Baptist:

And when Elizabeth heard the greeting of Mary, the babe leaped in her womb. (Luke 1:41)

Your Voice:

1. Instead of condemning young women in Mara Blake's situation, what can we do to help?
2. How can we support and help unwed mothers who choose to bring their pregnancies to term?
3. How can we help women who have had abortions and are haunted by guilt?
4. Should abortion be illegal?
5. Because of health, family, or social consequences, are there times in which abortion can be an option?
6. What would you do if you were in Mara's situation?
7. What can you do to avoid finding yourself in Mara's situation?

Chapter 15

WHAT DO I DO

If I Don't Graduate?

So, what're you going to do?" Travis asked.

"I've got to pass Finney's test," Manning responded. "If I don't, I'll flunk. And then I won't graduate." He gripped a brown paper towel and yanked it out of the rest room's dispenser.

"I can't believe Finney's being such a dork about it," Travis came back, "making such a big deal about one test when he knows it will stop you from graduating."

Manning swore and threw the paper towel on the floor. "My folks are making such a big thing about me graduating, too. Inviting everybody. If I don't pass this test, they'll go crazy."

"What about the Air Force?"

Manning crumpled another paper towel into a ball and

tossed it into the trash can across the room. "My recruiter'll go wild if I blow this."

Travis walked over to the large mirror, pulled a black comb out of his pocket and ran it through his hair. "You know," he said. "Finney was my gymnastics coach. He's a pretty good guy. I still go over to his house and joke around with him."

"So."

Travis put the comb back in his pocket, turned and faced Manning. "I might be able to get the answers to that test away from Finney," he said. "You can have 'em for fifty bucks."

Manning rolled his eyes. "Get serious."

"I am."

Manning shook his head.

"We're talking *graduation* here," Travis said, "and the Air Force."

"Naw, I don't think so."

"You gonna let Finney stop you from graduating? He's the one who's stickin' it to you. He knows how important it is. So stick it to him instead."

"I'd rather pass the thing on my own," Manning said, pulling his books off the lavatory shelf. "Besides, fifty's a lot of money."

"But it's worth it. *Graduation. Air Force.* And you'll burn Finney. Want to?"

"I don't know."

"C'mon. Where's your guts?"

"You don't even have the answers yet."

"But I can get 'em—easy."

What should Manning do?

Other Voices:

"You never could pass Finney's tests before. What makes you think you could pass this one?"

"Pay for that test and you'll be buying something that doesn't belong to you. You'd not only be cheating, you'd be stealing, too."

"Sometimes you've got to bend the rules for the goal you want to reach. You want to graduate, right? Well, that's too big a goal to let your conscience stand in the way."

"Buy those answers and get caught and I guarantee you won't graduate. Your safest bet is to study hard and do your best."

God's Voice:

God tells us clearly in the Bible that we "must not steal" (Exodus 20:15, TLB).

Your Voice:

1. Are there advantages to buying the answers from Travis?
2. Is cheating on a test the same as stealing?
3. What are some of the positive things Manning could do to make his graduation day a reality?
4. In the long run, would it be better for Manning to graduate with a guilty conscience by cheating, or to fail the test and not graduate with the rest of the class?

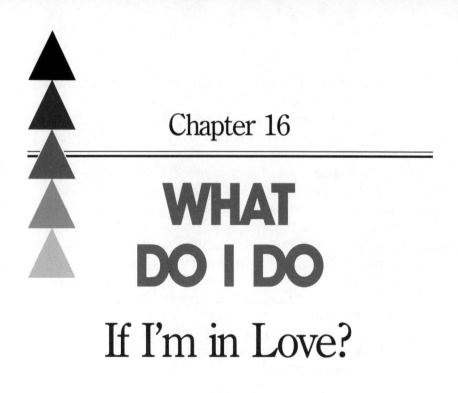

Chapter 16

WHAT DO I DO

If I'm in Love?

*C*ome with me," he said.

Something about him was mysterious, almost cruel. His face and body both frightened and delighted her. Billie knew the attraction she felt was dangerous, but she didn't care. He haunted her, obsessed her thoughts. She wanted to hold him and kiss him, maybe even go to bed with him. Thoughts of marriage had even crossed her mind.

She was in love.

"Whoa," he said, when she told him how she felt. "I'm not asking you to marry me. I'm just asking you to travel with me for a month. The carnival is heading to New Orleans, then on to Atlanta."

Billie laughed.

"Why are you laughing?" he asked, his voice rising above the sudden outburst of music from the merry-go-round.

"I could get into trouble," she smiled, her eyes flashing.

"Why? You just turned eighteen, didn't you? It'd just be for a few weeks. . . ."

Billie had met him last week when her church's youth group attended the carnival in the parking lot of a shopping mall. His name was Turk. She had bought cotton candy from him and they had struck up a conversation. He had impressed her by saying he was part owner of the entire carnival.

She was drawn to this man almost immediately. Yes, she had heard bad things about carnival people from her mother. But for some odd reason, right now, her mother's words were of little importance.

Billie went back the next day to see Turk. She spent all of Wednesday with him in his concession wagon. She even went to a movie with him on his day off.

Now, he was asking her to make a decision.

Every fiber in her body trembled. She knew she'd break her mother's heart and scandalize the church. Billie did not understand why, but she desperately wanted to say yes to Turk.

"Be here tomorrow morning at five," he said. "That's when we leave."

What should Billie do?

Other Voices:

"He's a carnie. You *know* what he's got on his mind."

"How romantic! Travel around the country with a guy like that. See all those cities. It'd be just like a movie."

"You think you're in love, Billie. But I call it infatuation. Being 'in love' is not the same as *love*. You're heading for big trouble."

God's Voice:

The Apostle Paul said:

I do not understand my own actions. For I do not do what I want, but I do the very thing I hate. (Romans 7:15)

The world has many definitions for love. But the Bible says:

God is love. (1 John 4:8)

You cannot truly love unless God is in your life. True love is like this:

Love is patient and kind; love is not jealous or boastful; it is not arrogant or rude. Love does not insist on its own way; it is not irritable or resentful, it does not rejoice at wrong, but rejoices in the right. Love bears all things, believes all things, hopes all things, endures all things. Love never ends. (1 Corinthians 13:4–8)

Your Voice:

1. Is there a difference between being "in love" with someone and "loving" someone?
2. Does the carnival worker's declaration of love match Paul's definition in 1 Corinthians 13?
3. How does real love operate in your life?
4. What would happen if Billie said yes to Turk?
5. How can we make sure we don't do what we "hate," even when we want to?
6. The Bible says, "God is love." What does this tell you about the nature of love?

Chapter 17

WHAT DO I DO

When I Can't Be What My Father Wants Me to Be?

*I*t was the moment Mike had dreaded.

Mike's father took his last bite of pizza, wiped his hands with a napkin, leaned back in his chair and lit up a cigarette. He blew out a large smoke ring which hovered over the kitchen table.

"Well, did you sign up. . . ?" Mike's father asked, resting both elbows on the table.

Mike's heart began pumping hard. "Uh—no," he said quietly.

"What's that?"

Mike felt sick. "No, sir," he said again, "I didn't."

Suddenly, his father violently crushed out the cigarette in an ashtray. He leaned forward, the blood rushing to his face.

74

"You mean you didn't sign up for football. . . ?"

"No, sir," Mike replied, his voice faltering. Old yearbook pictures of his father flashed into his mind. His father running for a touchdown . . . being elected the captain of the high school football team . . . receiving the Most Valuable Player trophy.

". . . But I'm going out for a fall sport all right . . ." Mike said hopefully.

"*What* fall sport?"

Mike said it, but no louder than a whisper.

"Would you speak up!" his father yelled.

"Cheerleading."

His father's fist slammed the table. "You've got to be kidding!" he shouted. "*Cheerleading?* That's for girls!"

"But Dad," Mike pleaded, "there're five guy cheerleaders in school and they all play baseball in the spring. . . ."

"I don't want to hear any more!" his father interrupted, rising abruptly to his feet. "After all I've told you about what football did for me when I was your age. . . ."

Then, he turned his back on his son.

But, Mike protested in his mind, *the guy cheerleaders practice at night, not when the football players practice. There won't be that many guys in the locker room. . . .*

Mike's father turned to face his son again. He pointed a finger in Mike's face. "You listen, and you listen *good.* Tomorrow you sign up for football. And I don't want to hear anymore about this cheerleading bunk."

But, Mike thought, *I've never liked football. Never could catch a pass. Never could take the hits. . . .*

"Do you understand me. . . ?" his father bellowed.

I'd have to take gang showers with seventy guys I don't know. They'd see that I'm not like them. My voice hasn't changed yet. I don't have hair on my body where they have hair. And I'm still smaller than the rest of them.

"*You're not answering me!*" Mike's father was livid.

"But Dad. . . ."

"I said I don't want any arguments! Are you signing up for football, or aren't you?"

Silence.

"Well?" his father demanded.

"Yes, sir," Mike said at last.

" 'Yes sir' *what?*"

"Yes, sir," Mike said as his stomach churned, "I will sign up for football."

What should Mike Benton do?

Other Voices:

"Just lie to him. Tell your old man you signed up, but then the coach cut you. Tell him you did your best."

"You think an ex-football jock like your dad would understand if you told him the real reason why you don't want to go out for football? Forget it. Keep it all to yourself."

"I know you really want to be a cheerleader, but you've got to forget about that. Don't even consider it. Your dad would make life miserable for you if you were a cheerleader."

"Go out for football. But try to mess up. Maybe you'll get cut. Or maybe you'll get injured."

"After all, he *is* your father. . . ."

"Maybe football won't be so bad. They might make a *real* man out of you after all."

"Forget your father. Do what you wanna do."

God's Voice:

The Bible tells us to obey our parents:

"Honor your father and your mother, that your days may be long in the land which the Lord your God gives you. (Exodus 20:12)

A father's hopes for a son may not always be the same as our heavenly Father's hopes for a son. But the Bible makes it clear that reasoning together, in respectful discussion, is a very good thing.

Your Voice:

1. What are some ways in which Mike can tell his father the real reason why he's afraid of going out for football?
2. What do you think Mike's father would say if he heard the true reason why Mike wants to be a cheerleader?
3. What if Mike's father explains that the main reason he wants Mike to go out for football is that he sincerely believes football will build Mike's character and prepare him for the future—and that is why he's making him go out for the team?
4. Do parents sometimes want you to be something you're not? What can you do about it?

Chapter 18

WHAT DO I DO

If I Don't Want to Be a Super-Christian?

*D*ear Diary,

Can't talk to anybody about this, not even God.

Last year, when I really decided to follow Jesus, it seemed my whole life changed. My parents made me go to church before that, but when it hit me Jesus was a REAL PERSON, I followed Him. And life was GREAT, to say the least. Really Great.

The problem is, I used to hang around with a bunch of druggies. Even though they were O.K. people, they were still druggies. I used to drink beer with them and smoke dope and do some other stuff I'm not too proud of. Then I decided I didn't need the stuff because I'd found Jesus, so I gave it up.

But now that I'm a Christian, I have to stay away from my druggie friends, because if I'm around them, they ask me if I want to do some flake. (My pastor said I should call it by its right name, otherwise I glamorize it.) If I turn it down, they'll ask me why I don't want cocaine any more. I'd say, "Because I follow Jesus." Most of them would laugh at me. And that hurt, because they were my FRIENDS.

I guess, now, I'd turn down coke or crack even if I wasn't a Christian, because it's bad stuff. But I used to go to parties, and on a Friday night there's only so many Bible studies I can go to. When my old friends are at a party and I'm not, sometimes I feel weird inside. Maybe I should just go to a party every now and then and drink one glass of vodka or something, and not make such a big deal about being a Christian. (Don't worry, I won't touch the flake.)

I guess what I'm saying is I think I should back off some on being a Christian. Maybe not be a Super-Christian, just a regular one. I know lots of adults who call themselves Christians and go to church, but they don't act spiritual all the time. I've seen them having a few drinks at wedding receptions. They don't always talk about the Lord, or worry about which friend of theirs is "unsaved." Maybe I want to be like those Christians, because to be an "on-fire Christian," like Pastor Moreau calls it, is too hard for me. I just can't do it anymore.

To be honest, I feel misled. Everybody says being a Christian is great, and I have to admit it is. But nobody ever told me how hard it was going to be. REAL HARD.

Other Voices:

"Even Jesus doesn't want you *not* to have fun. Why not go to a few parties?"

"If you go to those parties, they'll tempt you with booze and drugs. You may give in and destroy both your witness and your life."

"Hey, Jesus doesn't take people and change them into freaks. He takes freaks and changes them into people."

"Of *course* the Christian life is hard. So tough it out. Don't give up. It's eternally worth it."

"There are a lot of good Christians who *aren't* fanatics. . . ."

God's Voice:

Christ promised us many things, but never an *easy* life: "I come not to bring peace, but a sword." (Matthew 10:34, KJV).

He said, "The world will make you suffer," but fortunately He completed that statement, saying, "But be brave! I have defeated the world" (John 16:33b, GNB).

The Bible tells us the life of a Christian *is* demanding; it means *following* the risen Christ:

> Anyone who loves his father or mother more than me is not worthy of me; anyone who loves his son or daughter more than me is not worthy of me; and anyone who does not take his cross and follow me is not worthy of me. Whoever finds his life will lose it, and whoever loses his life for my sake will find it. (Matthew 10:37–39, NIV)

But despite hardship, the Bible tells us the life of a Christian is certainly a life of joy and purpose. Jesus himself said it is the best possible life:

> My purpose is to give life in all its fullness. (John 10:10, TLB)

The Holy Spirit of God will help us live the Christian life:

> You shall receive power when the Holy Spirit has come upon you. (Acts 1:8)

Your Voice:

1. How can a hard life be a good life?
2. For a Christian life to be truly "Christian," does it have to involve suffering?
3. Is temptation the same thing as sin? When does temptation become sin?

4. What is the difference between believing in Jesus and following Jesus?
5. Can you be a Christian without living a Christ-like life?
6. Why is it impossible to live a Christ-like life without God's help and grace?
7. Read Luke 4. How did Jesus handle temptation?
8. How do you deal with temptation?
9. What would you say to encourage the teenager who wrote this diary entry?

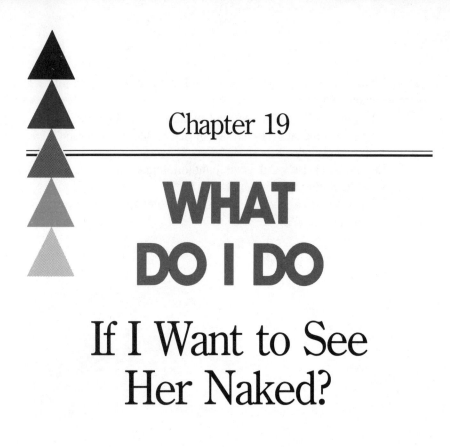

Chapter 19

WHAT DO I DO

If I Want to See Her Naked?

Look," Jet said, "it'll be simple."

"What do you mean?" Jim asked.

"She kind of likes to play around. You know, do stupid things. She's over in the woods at the end of the vacant lot. No one would see."

"I still don't know what you mean."

"She likes attention from older guys. I'll get my dad's yellow rope. We'll kind of goof around with her, you know. We'll ask her if she wants to play Rambo. She'll probably go for that, being younger and all. She can be Rambo's girlfriend. We'll be the enemies, and we'll tie her to a tree."

"Then what?"

"I'll pull up her shirt, you pull down her pants. We'll just get a look. Then we'll let her loose and tell her the game's over."

Jim couldn't believe what he was hearing. "She's still practically a kid. She's only in eighth grade. Forget it, Jet."

"But she *looks* older. She's built."

"No, it ain't right."

"C'mon. You want to see what a girl looks like with no clothes on, don't you?"

"Yeah, but not like this—not an eighth-grader."

"But she's *built* for her age. She probably looks like a lot of girls our age."

"We'll get into trouble."

"Don't give me that. You're dying to see her body too. Besides, she's got a crush on you. She won't mind. It'll make her feel good."

What should Jim do?

Other Voices:

"She'll think it's neat. You want to see her body."

"You could get in trouble with the law."

"She'll like it."

"I know you're curious about girls' bodies. You want to see a girl naked. But isn't there another way to satisfy your curiosity?"

God's Voice:

God created us male and female (Genesis 1:27). It makes sense that each sex will always be curious about the other. But Jesus said:

> If any of you causes one of these little ones who trusts in me to lose his faith, it would be better for you to have a rock tied to your neck and be thrown into the sea. (Matthew 18:6, TLB)

To abuse someone sexually or any other way is to damage their trust in God and in people. Jesus is severe in this warning, demonstrating that harming someone spiritually, emotionally, or sexually is a severe offense, causing extreme inner pain that could last a lifetime. The Word of God proclaims what modern psychology has recently discovered, that trauma in childhood can have devastating, long-term effects on a person.

Your Voice:

1. What damage could Jet's plan cause?
2. Is there another, less harmful way they could satisfy their curiosity about the female body?
3. Why do you suppose sexual or physical abuse is so devastating?
4. What can you do to protect yourself from sexual abuse?
5. How can you get help if a stepfather, uncle, aunt, neighbor, the person you babysit for, or someone else is sexually abusing you?
6. How can Christ heal your scars if you are a victim of sexual abuse?

Chapter 20

WHAT DO I DO

If My Teacher Says There is No Right or Wrong?

*W*hat do you mean you're going to back out?" Jared asked her as she drove him to the evening hearing at Groverton High School.

Sheri Blyers nervously ran the fingers of one hand through her hair. "Even if Mom wants to get rid of Mr. Filbright, I probably shouldn't be going to this meeting."

Groverton was a very conservative community. Recently, a touchy situation had come up involving one of the teachers, Mr. Filbright. Before Sheri knew it, she was at the center of a controversy that could cost a man his job.

It seemed that one of the school board members, Mr. See-dorf, had been talking to Filbright informally. During the conversation Filbright let it slip that he did not believe in absolutes—he did not believe that anything was necessarily right or wrong. Though he did not say so exactly, Filbright hinted that everything is relative; a person could lie, steal, murder, whatever, as long as the ends justified what he had to do.

Mr. Seedorf eventually told Sheri's mother, who was also a school board member, about their conversation. Mrs. Blyers was furious. She started a campaign to oust Filbright from Groverton High School. Anyone who had anything against Filbright jumped on her band wagon. She soon found it was legally difficult, if not impossible, to have Filbright fired. But if the pressure was poured on him, she reasoned, maybe he'd quit.

Tonight there was to be a special school board meeting at which kids were being asked to testify against Filbright, including Sheri.

It wasn't that Sheri's testimony alone would get Filbright fired—but it wouldn't help him either. If nothing else, the school would at last rid itself of its most unpopular teacher. The kids all hated him anyway.

"You *want* the dork to leave don't you?" Jared asked her. "You hate him as much as anyone else."

"Yeah, I do," Sheri said. She stopped fussing with her hair and adjusted the rear-view mirror for the third time. "But Mom says he's teaching kids there's no such thing as right or wrong. And I can't remember him saying anything like that in class."

"I can't either. But so what? He's a jerk. And he probably will say it in class some day."

"Jared, I can't go before that school board and *lie*. I never heard him say in class, 'There is no such thing as right and wrong.' "

"Maybe not. But remember how your mom asked you if he ever talked about abortion in class? Well, he *did* talk about abortion. He said some people feel under certain circumstances abortion is okay. Remember that? And didn't he say he thought that if a dying old man can't be helped you should let him die? Didn't he say that?"

"Yes. But he didn't teach us to believe either in abortion or in letting people die."

"C'mon, Sheri. What's the big deal? They're ready to get rid of the jerk anyway. Just tell 'em what they want to hear."

They drove into the school parking lot, and Sheri pulled into an empty space. The board meeting would start in minutes.

"You better not back out," Jared said. "Your mom and all the kids'll kill you."

What should Sheri do?

Other Voices:

"The man's got three kids. You don't want to get him fired. Tell the board Filbright may believe there are no absolutes, but that doesn't mean he teaches it to kids."

"How can you be a Christian and let a man who does not believe in an ultimate right or wrong mold young minds as a teacher in a public school?"

"Just don't go to the meeting. That way you wouldn't be helping him lose his job, but you wouldn't be helping him stay at his job either."

"If he doesn't believe in absolutes, he probably doesn't believe in God either. You've got to do whatever you can to keep Filbright from corrupting kids—even if it means stretching the truth a little."

God's Voice:

The Bible strongly affirms there are truths that are universally and absolutely true for all people for all time. Only in a few instances are commandments given to only a certain culture or to a certain set of circumstances.

The most important absolutes are these: the deity of Christ, salvation through faith in His death, and belief in the resurrection of Christ's body.

The Apostle Paul said:

I delivered to you as of first importance what I also

received, that Christ died for our sins in accordance with the scriptures, that he was buried, that he was raised on the third day in accordance with the scriptures, and that he appeared to Cephas, then to the twelve. (1 Corinthians 15:1–5)

For I the Lord do not change. . . . (Malachi 3:6)

However, nowhere do we read we should accuse a person fraudulently, despite what they may believe. In fact, one of the Ten Commandments says, "Do not accuse anyone falsely" (Exodus 20:16, GNB).

Your Voice:

1. Should a person who believes that "everything is relative" be allowed to teach in a public school?
2. If Christ is the "Truth" and if God does not change, what does this tell us about truth?
3. Can studying about philosophies that go against what the Bible says still be beneficial to us?
4. How was Jared being relative—ignoring the absolute truths—in his suggestions to Sheri?
5. Do you think allowing Mr. Filbright to teach is a threat to the students?
6. Understanding Exodus 20:16, what would you do if you were Sheri?
7. What should be taught in school? What should be taught in church?

Chapter 21

WHAT DO I DO

If I Told a Lie? (Even If It's Only a White One)

*H*e had everything written down on three index cards.

He read aloud what he would soon read over the telephone: "Hello Maria, this is Ben. . . ."

But what if she knows more than one Ben? he thought. *Better tell her my whole name.* "How're you doing. . . ?"

Can't I think of a better question to ask her than that? "Would you like to go to a movie on Saturday night? And maybe go out afterward for pizza?"

Ben checked over the other cards. If she said "yes," he had a special "yes card" to refer to, from which he read off a list of movies, times, and theaters—all while trying to sound casual. If she said no, he would consult a pocket calender and ask her if she could go to a movie on any other night. He decided to limit himself to suggesting only seven alternate dates. He figured if he went as high as seven without a positive response, then Maria had as good as told him to bug off.

Now he pulled out her phone number, written on the little card he'd kept in his wallet for months. His palms were sweaty. With trembling fingers he dialed the first number—the second. . . .

Will she laugh at me? he wondered, *Is she too good for me?* He kept dialing.

I don't have a chance. Better back out now. . . . But I'm sick of being the only guy without a date.

He dialed the last digit—but held the dial, afraid to let go. Finally he released it.

In a moment, he heard Maria's phone ring.

He hung up. After going through the whole, painful process once more, he bravely endured three rings. At last, he heard a female voice:

"Hello?" It sounded like her mother.

"Hello?" Ben said, his voice cracking. "Is Maria there?"

"Just a minute," she replied cheerfully.

But the wait seemed like forever. Again he hung up.

"I've got to talk to Jake," he told himself.

An hour later, Ben's best friend, Jake, was sitting across from him in his room.

"You want *me* to call up Maria and say I'm *you?*" Jake asked, disbelievingly.

"Sure. She knows my face and I think she knows my name, but not my voice. Besides, our voices sound kind of alike."

Ben headed out the bedroom door.

Jake picked up the receiver and started dialing. "Hey. Where are you going?" Jake called after him.

"I can't take it. I'm gonna wait in the hall. Let me know when it's over."

A few minutes later, Jake came out in the hallway, grinning. "It's on," he said. "I got you a date with Maria!"

Ben dated Maria not just once, but again and again. Of course, after that first time, he did his own phone-calling.

A year later Ben gave Maria his class ring. They were an inseparable couple. But Ben never told Maria he'd deceived her the first time he'd asked her out. She never knew it was really Jake she had talked to on the phone. And she made such a big deal about how much she liked Ben for his honesty. Other boys always lied to her, she told him. "They're cowards. They can't even tell the truth."

Should Ben tell her the truth about that first phone call?

Other Voices:

"This is stupid. Who cares? Don't tell her."

"What if she finds out some other way? Better tell her."

God's Voice:

Jesus said, "I am the Truth" (John 14:6).

Your Voice:

1. Is this a picky concern?
2. Should Ben tell Maria?
3. What reasons could Ben come up with for not telling Maria?
4. Is there such a thing as a "white lie"? What kind of habits can telling "white lies" lead to?
5. How can a friendship be harmed by lies?
6. Can you think of someone who has been severely hurt by lies told about him or her?
7. To be honest, do we have to tell people negative things about ourselves? Or are some things better left unsaid?
8. As long as Ben and Maria's relationship has blossomed, is it even important now to confront this matter?
9. How do you feel Maria will respond if Ben tells her the truth?
10. What does it mean to say Jesus is "the Truth"?

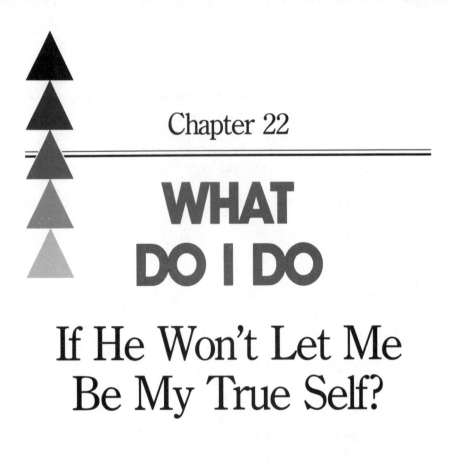

Chapter 22

WHAT DO I DO

If He Won't Let Me Be My True Self?

*T*amara always thought her body was shaped funny.

That's why she was amazed when Kyle showed an interest in her. It wasn't like they were going together or anything. Or that he had a crush on her, like she had on him. But Tamara thought it was better to live in a state of hopefulness than to have no one at all. They were very good friends.

But one day in class, a skinny, awkward woman from the local vocational school talked about all the programs available at her school. She said something about a couple of women in the mechanics program at the vo-tech.

Kyle laughed out loud from his seat in the back of the room.

"You may think it's funny," the woman shot back, "but we

get requests from some very large automotive firms for *female* mechanics."

"*Why?*" Kyle asked. And then he laughed again.

It was the laugh that cut into Tamara.

When her big brother had gotten his first car a few months back, Tamara helped him work on it by handing him the tools he needed. Soon she had grease on her hands and was doing actual work on the engine. Her brother taught her how to do all the mechanical work on her own motorcycle.

When this lady said women were enrolling in the auto mechanics program at the local vo-tech, something inside Tamara leaped for joy. But Kyle's laugh had killed that feeling. He was macho—one of those guys who thought women and girls should bake cookies because they were not good at much else. He would never understand. . . .

The lady from the vo-tech went on, "These automotive firms want women because they find females to be exceptionally good mechanics. Many women have superb dexterity. . . ."

Kyle was still snickering.

What should I do? Tamara wondered. *I want Kyle to like me, but his laugh scared me. I'll have to pretend I'm not interested in being a mechanic. . . . But I do want to be a mechanic.*

What should Tamara do?

Other Voices:

"You've got to be what you want to be."

"But you're so in love with him. You don't want to do anything that's going to keep him away from you. Especially now when he's showing more interest in you than ever before."

"You can't hide it. Let him know. Maybe he'll like you more for it."

"You want to keep him bad, don't you? Well, make sure you don't ever let him see grease under your nails."

God's Voice:

The Bible says that in Christ "there is neither Jew nor Greek, there is neither bond nor free, there is neither male nor female: for ye are all one in Christ Jesus" (Galatians 3:28, KJV).

Your Voice:

1. What should Tamara do?
2. Why did Kyle laugh at the idea of female mechanics?
3. Other than the obvious physical characteristics, what are the major differences between men and women?
4. Is there any job or occupation a woman should not do? A man?
5. What person is worth giving up a dream for?
6. What is your "real self"?
7. How can a Christian be true to his or her real self?

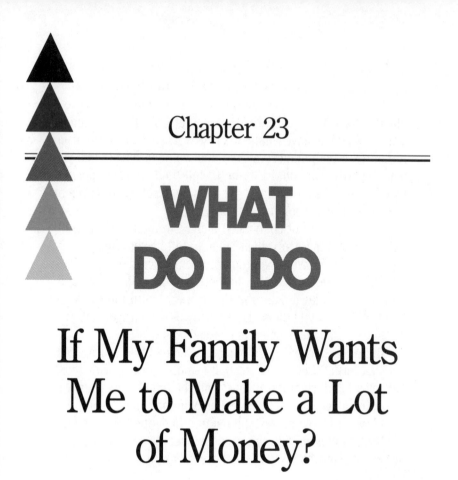

Chapter 23

WHAT DO I DO

If My Family Wants Me to Make a Lot of Money?

E very Wednesday, Elizabeth did volunteer work at the Sunshine Center, a facility for mentally handicapped children. She loved the children at the center, and was continually amazed at their depth and sensitivity. She even looked forward to Wednesdays in the summer. But there were times when the kids were hard to take. And now was one of those times. It made her wonder if she was doing any good by being here. So she decided to step outside for a moment and take a break.

Marilyn Anderson, the center's director, followed Elizabeth outside. She sat next to her on a picnic table.

"Elizabeth," Marilyn began, "you have a *gift*. You know that, don't you?"

"Oh . . ." Elizabeth said, caught off guard, "What's my gift?"

"You have a gift for working with the children in there," Marilyn said, pointing toward the center. "That's very important. Few people have what it takes to work with those children. It's an extremely important job, and we need people like you working with our kids, Elizabeth, full-time. Please consider working with us for a career. There's an excellent program at the vo-tech that would train you well."

Marilyn's vote of confidence made Elizabeth feel good inside. She couldn't wait to get home to tell her parents.

But when Elizabeth got home, she noticed her Aunt Sally had dropped in for a visit. Elizabeth's mother and Sally were both sitting on lawn chairs in the backyard with tall drinks in hand. Elizabeth told them about Marilyn's encouragement. Her mother smiled and seemed impressed.

But Aunt Sally gave a little smirk. She took a long drag from her cigarette. "Bethie," Aunt Sally said, "working with those kids may be all right for a while—maybe to help pay your way through college. But there's no money in that line of work. And I don't want to see my godchild starve to death." She smiled.

"*I won't starve*," Elizabeth said in anger. She was surprised at how strongly she felt about those kids at the center all of a sudden.

"Now, now," her mother cautioned.

"Bethie," Aunt Sally said condescendingly, "you may want to work with the retarded for a couple of years. But when you wake up to the *real* world, you'll find you want more money. *Please* go to college—not vo-tech—and get a *good* job."

"But working in the Sunshine Center is important work."

"Of course it is," Aunt Sally said. "But you can do equally important work and still make a decent living. Why don't you become a psychologist?"

"*Why don't you . . .*"

"Elizabeth," her mother interrupted, "I don't agree with everything your Aunt Sally is saying. But I do believe she deserves your attention—and respect," she added, sharply.

Now Aunt Sally looked directly at Elizabeth. There was anger in her voice. "It may sound harsh to tell you this, but I suppose now's as good a time as any for you to hear what I'm about to say. People who make as little money as you'll make at this Sunshine Center *aren't* looked up to by most people. In fact, they're looked down on. No, money isn't everything, but it's very, very important. Someday you'll agree with me."

What should Elizabeth do?

God's Voice:

The Bible does not say money itself is evil. But it does say:

For the *love* of money is the root of all evils; it is through this craving that some have wandered away from the faith and pierced their hearts with many pangs. (1 Timothy 6:10)

Money is necessary, but the world of money contains many traps. Jesus said, "Truly, I say to you, it will be hard for a rich man to enter the kingdom of heaven" (Matthew 19:23, NIV).

Your Voice:

1. Why is it that a lot of valuable work (such as work with children, or the handicapped, or the elderly) pays so little?
2. Can a person be wealthy and be a Christian at the same time?
3. How can you protect yourself from the "love of money" in such a materialistic age?
4. Does Elizabeth have an obligation to work with handicapped children because of her gifts?
5. Is poverty a virtue?

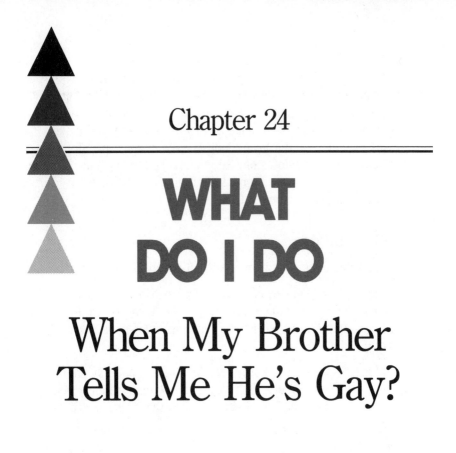

Chapter 24

WHAT DO I DO

When My Brother Tells Me He's Gay?

*T*he news slashed into Daryl.

He paced the yard in the darkness. Then in frustration he pounded his fist against the maple tree.

How can my own brother do this to me. . . ?

His brother, Mike, had asked the whole family—Dad, Mom, and their sister Jenny to come into the family room for a special announcement. That Mike had driven a hundred miles from college for this meant it must be important. Maybe he was engaged, Daryl had thought at first. But no—Mike hadn't been dating anyone seriously, not that Daryl knew. So they'd all gathered on the large sofa in the family room.

When Mike came in he was obviously nervous. His forehead was damp with sweat.

"I love all of you," he began. His face was tight, his voice shaky. Finally, after a long and agonizing pause, he said, "You may not understand what I'm about to say, but I ask you to please accept me and love me anyway."

Everyone glanced at each other, puzzled.

"Mom, Dad, Daryl, Jen—I'm gay. . . ."

Cold silence settled on the room.

"I'm *gay*," Mike repeated, his voice cracking. "And I'm tired of pretending I'm not."

Daryl's father groaned and covered his face with his hands.

"Dad," Mike implored, "these are modern times. I'm not *weird*. Look—you don't see horns growing from my head, do you?"

"But Mike . . ." his mother pleaded.

"I'm still your son, Mom. I'm gay, that's all."

"But you don't *look* gay," Jenny protested. She folded her arms tightly, and glared at him.

"What is this? The Inquisition? Look, I'm moving out of the dorm into an apartment with a guy named Jerry. He's gay too, Dad. Lots of the guys at college are. Please accept me, because I'm not going to change. I feel good about what I am."

Daryl jumped to his feet and shouted, "How could you? You taught me how to swim, how to throw a football! I've always looked up to you!"

Mike's eyes filled with tears. His voice trembled. "Can't you still look up to me? *I'm still your big brother.* I need to know you still love me—or at least *like* me."

Daryl stormed out of the house and slammed the door.

What should Daryl do?

Other Voices:

"There's nothing wrong with being gay. You have to accept Mike as he is, lifestyle and all."

"His kind is no good."

"The homosexual is a sinner. He breaks God's holy law

every time he commits a homosexual act. You need to tell your brother he's dead wrong, and that you cannot speak to him again until he gives up his sin."

"Just ignore him. I mean, he's your brother and all that, but it doesn't mean you have to hang around him all the time."

"Hey, is Mike hurting anybody? I figure if a guy picks a certain lifestyle and that lifestyle doesn't hurt anybody, then we can't judge. Right?"

God's Voice:

God has compassion on the person with a homosexual orientation, but every Bible passage about homosexuality soundly condemns gay sex acts:

> Do you not know that the unrighteous will not inherit the kingdom of God? Do not be deceived; neither the immoral, nor idolaters, nor adulterers, nor homosexuals, nor thieves, nor the greedy, nor drunkards, nor revilers, nor robbers will inherit the kingdom of God. (1 Corinthians 6:9–10)

Take careful note that homosexuals are not the only "unrighteous" on the list. Have you ever been greedy? Have you ever been immoral? No one should feel self-righteous.

> And as for others, help them to find the Lord by being kind to them, but be careful that you yourselves aren't pulled along into their sins. Hate every trace of their sin while being merciful to them as sinners. (Jude 23, TLB)

Another passage that Daryl should read to overcome self-righteousness is:

> For we ourselves were once foolish, disobedient, led astray, slaves to various passions and pleasures, passing our days in malice and envy, hated by men and hating one another; but when the goodness and loving

kindness of God our Saviour appeared, he saved us, not because of deeds done by us in righteousness, but by virtue of his own mercy, by the washing of regeneration and renewal in the Holy Spirit, which he poured out upon us richly through Jesus Christ our Savior, so that we might be justified by his grace and become heirs in hope of eternal life. (Titus 3:3–7)

One thing Daryl can do for his brother is to pray for him, because there are many dangers for the person who persists in habitual sin. And Daryl should also pray for himself.

First of all, then, I admonish and urge that petitions, prayers, intercessions, and thanksgivings be offered on behalf of all men. (1 Timothy 2:1, Amplified)

If you ask anything in my name, I will do it. (John 14:14)

Though we *all* sin, we are precious and deeply loved by God.

But God, who is rich in mercy, out of the great love with which he loved us, even when we were dead through our trespasses, made us alive together with Christ (by grace you have been saved). (Ephesians 2:4–5)

God loves the gay person, and longs to help everyone—gay or "straight"—overcome his or her sin.

But it's still important to remember that morality is infinitely more than trying to do what is right. Morality is Christ helping and empowering us to live biblically responsible lives as we walk in spiritual union with Him through prayer. We must seek union with Him daily.

And now just as you trusted Christ to save you, trust him, too, for each day's problems; live in vital union with him. Let your roots grow down deep into him and draw up nourishment from him. See that you go on growing in the Lord, and become strong and vigorous in the truth you were taught. (Colossians 2:6–7a, TLB)

Your Voice:

1. What would you do if you were Daryl?
2. If someone in your family announced he or she was gay, would it change your idea of homosexuality?
3. Why do you think all passages in the Bible dealing with homosexuality condemn gay sex acts?
4. If God loves gay people, how should you treat them?
5. What should Daryl do if Mike tells him he knows the Bible says gay sex acts are wrong, but that it's not going to change his lifestyle?
6. How can we love a person and not condone that person's sins? How can we not condone a person's sins without appearing self-righteous?
7. Read John 7:53; 8:11. What would Jesus say to the woman if she were a lesbian?
8. If you are tempted to participate in a gay sex act, or are suddenly overcome by strong sexual feelings for a member of your own sex, what should you do?
9. What is the difference between having affection for a member of your own sex and having a homosexual orientation?
10. Does the person who has the desire to participate in a gay sex act, but refuses to do so, fall under the "unrighteous" category of 1 Corinthians 6?
11. If true morality is believing that Christ lives within you through the Holy Spirit, and that he can empower you to live a biblically responsible life, how does this work, practically speaking?

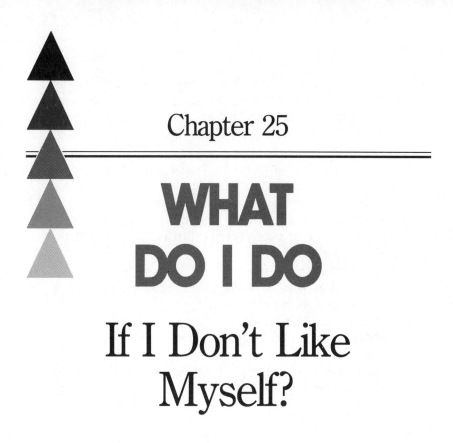

Chapter 25

WHAT DO I DO

If I Don't Like Myself?

*T*he heavy school doors shut behind Matthew Sherman. He and his mother and father moved through the jostling crowd of noisy students until they reached the principal's office.

Matt was terrified. New school. New faces. New cliques. And he was the new student.

"We're happy to have you here, Matt," said Mr. Bozeman, the principal, from behind his cluttered desk. He extended a clammy handshake.

But I'm not happy to be here, Matt thought.

Mr. Bozeman explained to Matt and his parents what the school's student guidelines were, using a little red booklet. When that was done and the adults were chatting, Matt excused himself to go to the rest room.

In the principal's outer office, a very nice-looking girl was talking to the school secretary. She was about Matt's age, with tanned skin and striking blond hair. He thought her earrings and bracelets were probably real gold. When he said "hi," she ignored him.

Once inside the lavatory, he looked down at his tennis shoes. They were old and out-of-style.

"What am I doing here," he said out loud.

His folks had lost their farm, and his dad had just gotten a job in the city. So Matt wasn't even called a farm boy any more. He felt like a nothing.

He looked in the mirror.

His face was so plain. Not like the smooth, tanned faces. A face so poor—crawling with pimples.

"I hate you," he whispered.

But what can I do about it? I can't change myself, he thought.

The bell rang. His heart filled with horror as he listened to the flood of voices in the distant hallways. All those city kids out there. . . .

What should Matt do?

Other Voices:

"Of course you can change yourself. Buy some new clothes. Borrow the money if you have to. Pay a little more for a decent barber. Go to the doctor and see if there's something you can do about your face."

"Who says you can't make it here? You're a human being, aren't you? Doesn't every human being in this country have the opportunity to make it in life?"

"Give up. Might as well quit school. You don't have a chance."

God's Voice:

We are to love our neighbor *as we love ourselves* (Matthew 22:39). It's important to love yourself, no matter what you look

like, who you are, or what you've done in the past.
God loves you so much He sent Jesus Christ to die for you.

> God . . . did not even keep back his own Son, but offered him for us all! He gave us his Son—will he not also freely give us all things? (Romans 8:32, GNB)

Your Voice:

1. When does self-love become self-worship? What are the potential dangers of self-love?
2. Why should you love yourself?
3. Have you ever felt like Matt Sherman? Why?
4. How do you think God sees you?
5. In what ways can you show love to yourself?
6. What can Matt do to make his situation easier?

Chapter 26

WHAT DO I DO

If My Best Friend Wants Nothing to Do With Me?

*T*he two young women stepped out of the car. One of them carried a cooler in her arms. The other followed, carrying a blanket.

Soon, the blanket was spread out on the sandy beach. Gulls circled overhead. The two young women sat cross-legged. One of them lit up a cigarette and then opened the cooler. She pulled out a can of beer, yanked the tab, and rushed the can to her lips as the foam gushed out. Then she handed the can to the other young woman, Brenda Merril.

Brenda shook her head.

"What's the matter?" her friend asked. "They teach you not to drink beer at that Bible camp, too?"

"Look, Kim," Brenda said, "I learned about Christ at camp. *That's all.*"

"So? Does this mean you can't have a little fun?"

Brenda reluctantly took the can. She sipped it. "Beer isn't always fun," she said. "I can drink *one* of these. But I better not drink more. More than one and next thing you know, I'm doing things I don't want to do. Like driving while I'm blitzed."

"But that's what's so great about drinking," Kim said, flicking her cigarette butt to the sand. "It's so risky. You never know what this stuff'll make you do. And that makes it fun. . . ."

"Well, since coming home from camp, I've got better things to do," Brenda said, taking another bird-like sip of beer.

Kim gave her a wicked glint. "Do you think I'm going to hell?"

"I never said that," Brenda objected.

"Yeah, but I'll bet you *think* it—just because I'm not on the same religious kick you are."

Brenda looked away from her, following the movement of the gulls with her eyes as they swooped just above the surface of the lake. "All I know," she said, "is if you don't follow Jesus. . . ." And her voice trailed off lamely.

Suddenly, Kim rolled on her back, kicked her legs up in the air and laughed out loud. "I don't believe it!" she roared.

Brenda stood up and threw her beer can into the sand. "Quit laughing at me!" she protested. "God's the only one who can tell you. . . ."

Now Kim was on her feet, cutting Brenda off. "Ever since you came back from camp, you've been treating me like I'm a criminal or something. What's the matter? You too good for me now?"

She picked up her cooler. "We've been friends all these years, and I've always stuck by you. Just last month, Leslie said she wasn't going to invite you to her party, because she thinks you're boring. But *I* talked her into inviting you. Now you tell me I'm going to hell."

"I didn't say that . . ."

Kim turned her back and started walking away, lugging her

blanket and beer cooler. "I can hitch-hike home," she said.

"Oh come on, Kim," Brenda said, trailing after her. "I'll drive you home if you're really that angry at me."

"Forget it," Kim snapped. "If you think I'm going to hell, then I don't even care to see you anymore. You stink."

The gulls circled overhead as Brenda watched her friend retreat across the beach.

What should Brenda do?

Other Voices:

"Hey, after all she's done for you, compromise a little for the sake of your friendship."

"Well, if she treats you that way, she can take a hike."

"What kind of Christian are you, acting like you're better than Kim?"

God's Voice:

Don't be teamed with those who do not love the Lord, for what do the people of God have in common with the people of sin? How can light live with darkness? And what harmony can there be between Christ and the devil? How can a Christian be a partner with one who doesn't believe? (2 Corinthians 6:14–15, TLB).

Your Voice:

1. Should Brenda compromise to keep her friendship?
2. Is Kim a true friend?
3. What would you do if you were Brenda?
4. How can Brenda show Christian love to Kim even though they may no longer have similar interests?

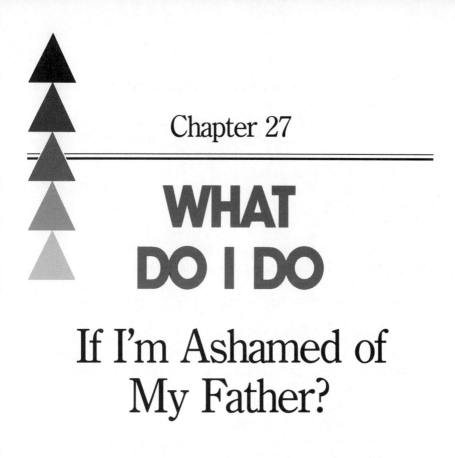

Chapter 27

WHAT DO I DO

If I'm Ashamed of My Father?

*T*he music pulsated throughout his entire being.

Shane's long and slender fingers slid up and down the strings of his guitar as he performed from the stage. The music filled the gym.

His bluegrass band was somehow reaching the souls of all the kids at the school, though bluegrass was by no means popular there. Maybe it was because the kids were relieved to get out of school during homecoming week to hear a concert given by their fellow students. At any rate, Shane loved all the long-awaited attention.

Suddenly, a movement caught his eye. He couldn't believe what he was seeing.

The short guy waddled across the gym floor. At that moment he looked like such an old man.

My father! Shane's mind raced with panic as the twanging music burst from the band's guitars and banjos. *His sloppy factory clothes. His bald head. His crazy laugh. Chomping on bubble gum. What's he doing here?*

His father had always said, "Why don't you go out for football or something? So I could come up to the school and see you play and be proud?"

. . . The music was over.

Shane and the other guys in his band were packing up their instruments and equipment. His father still sat over on one of the bleachers, as he had for over an hour, waiting for Shane to talk to him.

Shane had never had to introduce the guys to his father. His house was a dump compared to theirs, so he never brought them home. He figured his father wasn't as young or as smart or as wealthy as their fathers.

Now his father sat there, beaming at him proudly, waiting to be acknowledged as his dad.

But Shane could only think of ducking out the side door.

What should Shane do?

Other Voices:

"You introduce your old man to the rest of the guys and he'll tell them some stupid joke, or he'll talk about Vic Damone and the music he used to listen to when he was young. He just got off his sweaty job and he didn't even have time to shower, so he probably smells bad. He'll embarrass you."

"He's your own father. And you're ashamed of him?"

"All the other guys have Dads who are insurance executives or doctors. If they knew the kind of dad you had, they'd disown you. Cut out."

"Your Dad loves you. He got out of work to come see you.

He's proud. The least you could do was thank him and introduce him to the other guys."

God's Voice:

I bid every one among you not to think of himself more highly than he ought to think. . . . (Romans 12:3)

Your Voice:

1. Have you ever felt embarrassed because your parents showed up at one of your social occasions?
2. Did Shane feel he was better than his father?
3. Why do some people think they are better than other people?
4. What kind of father was Shane's father?
5. What can you do to not think too highly of yourself?

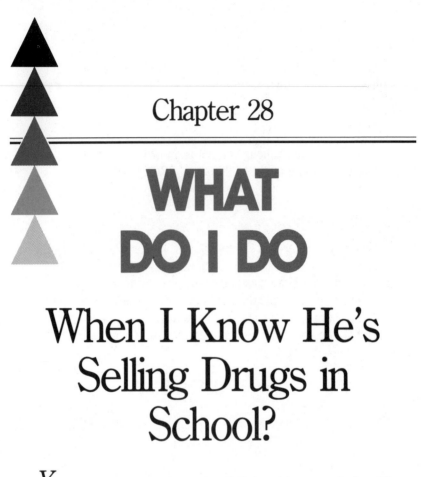

Chapter 28

WHAT DO I DO

When I Know He's Selling Drugs in School?

You better shut up about this," Nelson threatened, "or I'll bash in your head!"

Mason felt the sensation deep within his belly. It felt like something shaking and rattling. He looked at Nelson's "friend"—a young guy in dark glasses with a stubbly beard. Nelson's words stuck in him like sharpened darts hurled full-force.

"Don't worry about *this* geek," Nelson said, referring to Mason. The guy in the dark glasses stood behind the open locker door, which acted as a shield. "He won't tell nobody," Nelson concluded.

A slow smile crawled across the guy's stubbly face. "Good. So you won't give us no trouble?" he asked Mason.

Mason stood next to his own locker, clutching his biology book. He swallowed. Then he tried to speak, but the words would not come.

"I don't hear you talking" the guy persisted. He was no longer smiling.

But the words would still not come out.

"I told you he won't be no trouble," Nelson insisted.

"*Shut up!* I want to hear it from *him*." The guy started toward Mason. "You don't see *nothin'*, right?"

"Right," Mason said at last.

Then he turned his back on them. It made no difference. He knew what would happen next. The guy would hand Nelson a bag of coke, or some other drug. Nelson would slip the guy a roll of cash. The drugs would go into Nelson's locker.

"You keep your mouth shut about this, geek," the guy said. He walked away quickly.

What right does he have to threaten me? Mason thought angrily. *What right does he have to be in this school?*

But every Thursday, he saw the guy slip into the school—unnoticed by teachers and the administration. He'd appear as if by magic at Nelson's locker, hand him the bag, and Nelson would give him the cash.

Then they would both look at Mason and laugh.

"Don't worry about the geek," Nelson would laugh. "Geek . . . geek . . . geek . . ."

And each week Mason could see Nelson becoming more unkempt, more wasted.

"Geek! He won't tell no one!"

What should Mason do?

Other Voices:

"Are you *crazy*? Tell? Every druggie in town would be after your neck."

"He's breaking the law. Tell the police."

"But if he got in trouble, the guy'd suspect you right off."

114

"They think you're too much of a coward to tell. At least report it for your own self-respect. At least tell the principal."

God's Voice:

Do not be afraid, but speak and do not be silent; for I am with you, and no man shall attack you to harm you; for I have many people in this city. (Acts 18:10)

Your Voice:

1. In the above Bible passage God told the Apostle Paul he had "many people in this city," so Paul need not be afraid. Do you feel that if Mason reported the drug deals, people would stand beside him?
2. Does the above passage promise that Mason would not get beat up if he reported the drug deals? Or is such thinking a faulty application of scripture?
3. If Mason reports the drug deals, what do you think will happen?
4. If Mason gets beat up for reporting the deal, what should he do then?
5. If Mason is too afraid to report the drug deal, are there still some things he can do to improve the situation?
6. What would you do if you were Mason?
7. How can students bind together to protect their school from drugs?
8. In what ways does God protect us?

Chapter 29

WHAT DO I DO

If I Can't Be Kind to Him?

*T*he two boys could still hear the laughter and the cheers from the church gym as they snuck away up the back stairs.

It was Sunday evening—"Youth Fellowship Night." But Farraday and Stecker had slipped out of the crowded gym during the dodge ball game. This was the real reason they came to Youth Fellowship, to run around the large church and sneak into offices.

Stecker tried the pastor's office door. It opened! The boys snuck in, feeling as if they were entering a forbidden zone. Stecker switched on the desk light. He sat in the black swivel chair behind the desk, and Farraday perched on the desk itself.

Stecker picked up the telephone receiver and, one by one, called up four of the prettiest girls from school. When each one

116

answered, he whispered some obscenities and quickly hung up. Then he and Farraday would roar with laughter.

In a few minutes, Stecker said, "Let's call that faggot, Billy."

Billy no longer came to Youth Fellowship because people like Stecker and Farraday tormented him.

But tonight, for some odd reason, Farraday felt a little guilty.

"Naw," he said, "let's not."

"C'mon, pansy."

"Naw, let's get outta here."

Stecker's hand reached out and pinched Farraday's cheek. "What's the matter? Don't want to hurt your *sweetheart's* feelings?"

Suddenly, Farraday felt a little trapped. He knew Stecker could be vicious.

"He'll know it's us," Farraday argued.

"So what? You pick up the extension on that other desk over there. I'll dial the number."

Reluctantly, Farraday gave in. In a moment, he could hear the phone ring at the other end.

A deep voice answered—Billy's father.

"Ah, hello. Is William there?" Stecker asked, with a choir boy's innocence.

"Just a minute."

I can't be kind to Billy, Farraday thought. *Kids'll think I like him. They may think I'm like him if I'm kind. . . .*

"Hello?"

"Hi, William!" Stecker greeted. Then his voice became purposely high-pitched. He sang out, "My name is Feminine Billy, and I'm a great big fag. I walk like a girl and talk like a girl, and I dress in drag. . . . Now a word from my assistant. Why don't you say something, assistant?"

"Who is this?" Billy demanded.

Farraday opened his mouth, but no words would come.

"C'mon assistant, *say something to your sweetheart.*"

Farraday was about to whisper, "Faggot." But before he could, Billy hung up.

Stecker looked at him. "Am I mistaken—or is it really true love? Back on the phone, Farraday, or else I'll tell all the guys about you and Billy." And he winked.

What should Farraday do?

Other Voices:

"This is a church. How can you use a church phone to crucify another human being?"

"Tell Stecker you were going to call Billy a faggot, but he hung up too fast. You don't want Stecker to think you *like* Billy, do you?"

"He's a human being like you. With real feelings that hurt just as easily as yours."

"His type is no good. Maybe by leaning on him a little you'll give the message he'd better start acting like a guy, not a girl."

"Jesus loves Billy. A Christian had better love him too."

God's Voice:

And be kind to one another, tenderhearted, forgiving one another, as God in Christ forgave you. (Ephesians 4:32).

Your Voice:

1. Can Farraday be kind to Billy without identifying with him? How?
2. Even if other people think Farraday is like Billy by being kind to him, does this mean Farraday should *not* be kind to him?
3. What is a "true man"? A "true woman"?

4. How can Farraday lessen the damage done to Billy?
5. What should Farraday say to Stecker?
6. How can you show kindness and love to people you don't like or agree with?

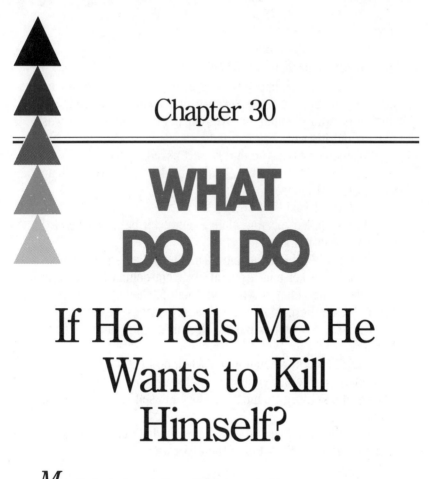

Chapter 30

WHAT DO I DO

If He Tells Me He Wants to Kill Himself?

*M*orris had always figured Bert was odd.

Bert was a born actor. It was during the class play, when Bert was playing the part of a clown and Morris a policeman, that they got to know each other. You couldn't really say they became friends, because they never went to play video games together, or to cruise around town. But they did become acquaintances.

They'd talk to each other at school, laugh and joke. And Morris liked Bert. He enjoyed seeing him act out his many different roles in school. He enjoyed hearing him sing like an opera star in the showers after phy ed or talk like Pee Wee Herman in study hall. It was fun to hear him give a monologue like some stand-up comedian when he was supposed to give an impromptu speech in English.

Morris even thought Bert was pretty funny on the day he came up to him between seventh and eighth hour and told Morris he was planning on dying next week. He said he was making out his will.

"Would you like to be in it?" Bert asked Morris.

"In what?" Morris asked, leaning against the Coke machine in the student lounge.

"My will, I said."

Morris smiled, playing along. "Sure. I'll be in your will. I get your beautiful sister."

"You got her!" Bert beamed. Then he pulled a note pad out of his back pocket and a pencil out from behind his ear. He scribbled something down, and then flashed a mysterious smile. "When I croak, you can have my sister," he said.

The next day Morris passed Bert in the hall on his way to lunch.

"Hey!" Morris greeted him. "When do I get your sister?"

But Bert was not smiling now. In fact, he wore a look of deep sadness. In a moment, he lost himself in the crowded lunchroom.

The following week, Morris found a whole box of compact disks in his locker. On top of the disks was a note.

Morris,
Please accept these gifts from one actor to another.

Morris was dumbfounded. The disks had to be some of Bert's most prized possessions. Why give them away? But when he questioned Bert about it, Bert looked past Morris and shrugged. "I don't know. In case I leave suddenly . . . I thought you would enjoy 'em."

The next day, Morris stopped to talk to Bert in front of the concession stand at the basketball game.

"What have you been up to lately?" Morris asked.

"Oh, figuring out how to hang myself," Bert said crazily, in a high voice like Mickey Mouse.

That night, as Morris walked home, he knew that the actor

who had given away all his compact disks was going to kill himself.

What should Morris do?

Other Voices:

"Don't jump to any hasty conclusions. He's an actor, just playing another part, that's all."

"Call the suicide crisis center."

"He's just going through a rough time now. Leave him alone. He'll get over it."

"You've got to confront him. Ask him if he's going to do it. If he says yes, talk him out of it."

"He's just joking around."

"Tell the school counselor."

"Tell him what a great guy he is. Tell him you'd miss him if he were to go away."

God's Voice:

Carry each other's burdens. (Galatians 6:2)

Your Voice:

1. God loves Bert with all His heart. God has a special plan for his life and would therefore be very sad, as would countless others, if Bert did something harmful to himself. How would Bert respond or feel if he were told this truth?
2. Do you think Bert is going to kill himself, or is he just playing a part?
3. Can Morris afford *not* to take Bert's threat seriously?
4. Even if Bert is not serious about suicide, why would it be good for Morris to tell him the "truth" that God has a special plan for his life anyway?

5. What would you do if you were Morris?
6. If Bert does kill himself, who's to blame? Should Morris blame himself?
7. What plan of action can you work out to be prepared in case a friend tells you he or she is contemplating suicide?

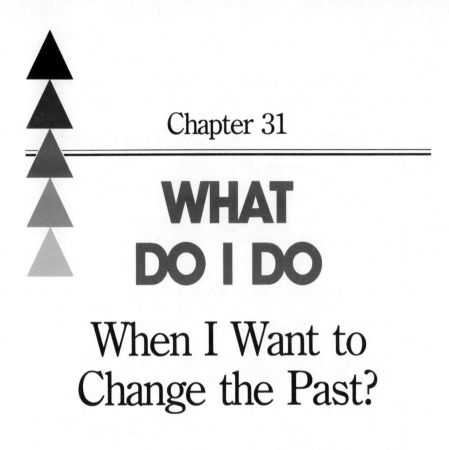

Chapter 31

WHAT DO I DO

When I Want to Change the Past?

Mara Blake could see him in the rear-view mirror.

There stood Todd, right in the middle of her driveway. He was in uniform and must have come directly from the army base.

Mara started the car, put it in reverse and backed up.

Todd dodged the car. "Hey!" He yelled. But she snapped down the lock on the driver's door just as he lunged for the handle.

"I need to talk to you!" he called through the window. But she shook her head at him. As she backed into the street, he sprinted around to the other side of the car. Mara tried to stretch across the front seat to lock the passenger's door, but Todd got there first.

To her dismay, he pulled open the door and slid in next to her. Stiffly, she straightened up and put the car in park.

Both of them were silent for a long time.

"When did you get back from Germany?" she asked, finally.

"Early this morning," he said. Then, "Mara, why? Why did you do it?" His voice cracked.

She could not answer. She'd been numb for weeks.

"Talk to me," he pleaded. "*Why?*"

She wanted to say so many things. She wanted to explode in rage. Thousands of cruel and sad thoughts flooded her mind. At last, she just broke into tears.

Tears streamed down Todd's cheeks, too.

"Why'd you do it?" he blurted out again.

"Why don't you say the word, Todd?" she said ferociously. "Why don't you ask me why I got an *abortion?*"

"Okay. . . !"

"The baby *belonged* to *me*," she said.

"But why didn't you tell me you were pregnant?"

Mara just bent over the steering wheel. She continued to cry.

"You did what *you* wanted to do. So why are you crying?" Todd asked bitterly.

She straightened up. "Don't I have a right to be sad? Don't I have a right to cry? I'll never hold my baby."

He turned away from her, looking out the window. Sad thoughts stabbed him.

If only I could change the past, he thought. *Go back to that night in the motel. Change the outcome. . . .*

The motor hummed.

The baby's dead. . . . The baby's dead. . . !

What should Todd do?

Other Voices:

"Hate her. Call her a killer. She deserves it."

"Change the past? Don't be ridiculous."

"Drive it all out of your mind. Don't think of the little boy or girl who was aborted. Think of the child you'll have one day."

"Lighten up, would you? None of it's *your* fault."

"It takes two to tango. It's your fault, too."

God's Voice:

No one has the power to go back in time and physically change what happened in the past. But incredibly, God, in Christ, will "justify" us (Romans 8:33)—restoring us to righteousness—if we turn to Him, asking Him to forgive us because of Jesus.

To be "justified" means to be made just-as-if-we-had-never-sinned. God can justify us in spite of our past. So, in a spiritual sense, the past *can* be changed through Christ's dealing with our sins.

You see, the Bible states that Jesus, God's own Son, was punished in our place for our sin, so we will not have to be punished. In Christ, God has cast our sins away from us. And Jesus died in our place, so we who believe in Him do not have to suffer eternal separation from God when we die.

As Paul said,

He who did not spare his own Son but gave him up for us all, will he not also give us all things with him? Who shall bring any charge against God's elect? It is God who justifies; who is to condemn? Is it Christ Jesus who died, yes, who was raised from the dead, who is at the right hand of God, who indeed intercedes for us? Who shall separate us from the love of Christ? (Romans 8:32–35a)

You don't have to clean yourself up before turning to Christ. Jesus himself said:

Come to me, all who labor and are heavy laden, and I will give you rest. Take my yoke upon you, and learn from me; for I am gentle and lowly in heart, and you will find rest for your souls. For my yoke is easy, and my burden is light (Matthew 11:28–30)

God can take even the bad things in our lives and, when we surrender ourselves to Him, use them for good:

We know that in everything God works for good with those who love him, who are called according to his purpose. (Romans 8:28)

Cast all your anxiety on him because he cares for you. (1 Peter 5:7, NIV)

God will also help us as we live our lives:

Likewise the Spirit helps us in our weakness. (Romans 8:26)

Your Voice:

1. Is there a sin that God will not forgive?
2. By forgiving sin and working bad things into good, does God, in a sense, change the consequences of the past?
3. Can you think of any ways your past has been changed by God's forgiveness?
4. If you were the only person in the world who had ever sinned, would God still send Christ to die for you?
5. How would you comfort Todd and Mara?

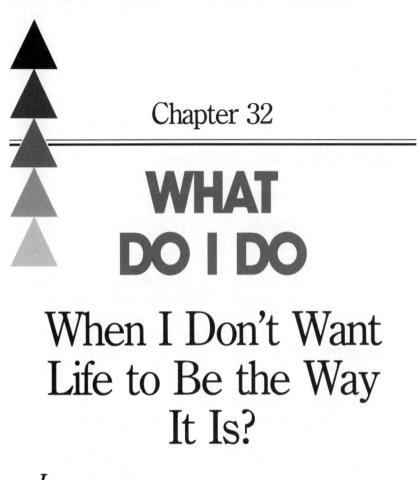

Chapter 32

WHAT DO I DO

When I Don't Want Life to Be the Way It Is?

*J*essica Palmer poised herself in the starting blocks. The 100-meter dash would begin with the crack of the starter's pistol.

Now Jessica kicked a leg back to position herself just right, her fingers touching the warm blackness of the track. . . .

When she'd started this track season, life was bubbling within her as she carried around a joy that she took for granted because she had no reason *not* to take it for granted. Jessica had never been out for a sport before, but she figured she'd better go out for track this year, because at Paramount High School, you were a goddess if you could shine on an athletic team—and a social outcast if you couldn't. Coach Baker was impressed with her speed. And Jessica had received second- or third-place ribbons in a number of races. . . .

"Set!" the starter cried out as he raised his pistol straight up in the air. Jessica leaned forward, putting the full weight of her body upon her arched finger tips. . . .

But as the season had trudged on, Jessica at last discovered the world of track and field was not what her dreams had anticipated it would be. The drudgery of the long and hard workouts in the hot sun, the snarling jealousy of her teammates who were also desperate for athletic recognition. . . .

Gun shot!

Jessica now dove out of the blocks. Her flat spikes tore into the track as her opening strides lifted her from a crouch to a standing run. . . .

Because track wasn't what she dreamed it would be, Jessica had thought of quitting. But the attention she was getting was too hard to give up. Now as her ears were bombarded by the thunder of pounding feet and the cheering of the crowd in the distance, and her eyes drank in the flashing colors of all the representative schools, she thought maybe, despite the glory, it wasn't really worth it after all.

And there was something more.

A month ago, her whole concept of life had changed. It had all happened in one week.

First, her boyfriend, Al, told her he had lost his virginity at thirteen. Then Jessica found out that her pastor, a family man whom she admired very much, was having an affair with a realtor. And finally, the bombshell—Jessica's mother and father told her they were getting separated. Jessica had seen this coming for a long time, but she had never believed it would actually happen.

Why can't life be the same as it was before? Thoughts screamed through her head as she reached the 50-meter mark. To her surprise she was dead even for first place with a sprinter from Carlyle High School. Her coach always told her this was the point of the race where she'd be close to her peak. All it would take is a little extra push. . . .

Am I the only idiot whose holding onto my virginity? Is there a moral adult left anywhere? Do any marriages last forever?

Arms pumped. Feet hammered the track.

The extra push! All it would take is the extra push! Could she. . . ?

The race was over.

Jessica finished last.

She walked to the locker room. There she turned in her spikes and uniform. She left the stadium and drove home, never to return.

But what would she do about her life?

Other Voices:

"Life stinks."

"Smile. Don't let your face be long. There's still a lot of life to be happy about."

"Life will *never* be the same again. You've got to quit thinking like a kid. Start thinking like an adult. The good times are gone."

"Life is ultimately good, not bad, and therefore worth living."

God's Voice:

The Bible tells us many times God is good (Psalm 73:1).

My health fails; my spirits droop, yet God remains! He is the strength of my heart; he is mine forever. (Psalm 73:26, TLB)

Despite problems, sufferings, tragedy, and evil, life *is* worth living because God is good. God loves this world, though you may hate it.

For God so loved the world, that he gave his only begotten Son, that whosoever believeth in him should not perish, but have everlasting life. For God sent not his Son into the world to condemn the world, but that the world through him might be saved. (John 3:16–17, KJV)

Your Voice:

1. Can you ever regain the joys of yesterday?
2. In what ways is life worth living? In what ways is life good?
3. How can you increase your awareness of the beauty of life and the love God has for you?
4. What can Jessica do about her troubles?
5. What should you do if someone you know is talking about suicide?

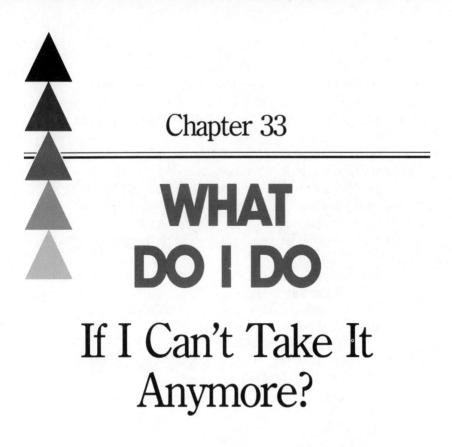

Chapter 33

WHAT DO I DO

If I Can't Take It Anymore?

*T*he last bell of the day.

The laughter and the shouting. Then, the hollow and empty hall. The school always cleared out quickly on a spring afternoon.

But Callie could not take it any more.

She told them that if they pushed her too far, she'd run away. It was a promise, and she always stuck to her word.

She looked at the books piled at the bottom of her locker. *Books?* And then she almost laughed at the absurdity of the situation. *Why worry about homework now?*

No teacher or counselor or principal seemed to understand why Callie had difficulty concentrating on Math or English or Social Studies. But what good was it to even go to school when you're always thinking about how messed up your life is?

Callie slammed her locker door and the sound rang down the empty halls. Her life felt as hollow and as empty as the echo.

I can't go home. I'm afraid of him, she thought. *He's not my father just because he married Mom.*

She took a step backward from her locker and looked right and then left down the long and empty hall.

Does a father scream at you and call you names so rotten you want to die? Does he always say you're "no good"? Or call you a dirty, little tramp?

She walked down the hall. She could do it. They wouldn't miss her till she was long gone.

He slaps me night after night. And then he beats me!

She started running down the hall.

Got to get away from home...!

But what about your mother? another voice argued inside her. *Her heart'll break if you run away....*

She doesn't act like my mom anymore, always sides with him.

But she loves you....

No! Not anymore, she loves him now.

Now she was out on the sidewalk, her thoughts still racing....

I'll go to San Francisco, I've got friends there.

But when the money runs out, where will you find a job?

When Callie reached her car, she could only stand and stare.

Home? It wasn't home anymore. But her mother was all she had.

The road? Away from *him*. But the road looked full of danger.

Home? Beaten into the floor with his ugly words. Beaten on the arms, and even on the face....

But where would she spend tonight?

Home? Or the road?

What should Callie do?

God's Voice:

Cast all your anxieties on [the Lord], for he cares about you. (1 Peter 5:6)

Jesus said:

Whatever you ask in my name, I will do it, that the Father may be glorified in the Son; if you ask anything in my name, I will do it. (John 14:13–14)

Your Voice:

1. If Callie were to trust God to help her in this situation, what do you think God would have her do?
2. Which is the best option for Callie—running away, or staying at home?
3. The two options are not ideal solutions. Is there an "in-between" course of action she can take?
4. What are the dangers of running away? Of living in an abusive home?
5. If Callie were to ask God to help her in Christ's name, how do you think God would help her?
6. What would you tell Callie if she asked you for advice?
7. Who are some people Callie can turn to for help?

Chapter 34

WHAT DO I DO

If My Religion's Driving Me Crazy?

*H*is handshake was firm—to the point of being bone-crushing!

Collin Pense wiggled his fingers a little bit, and then sat down in a chair in front of the lawyer's desk. The lawyer reached into an upper desk drawer, pulled out a large, black Bible and plopped it down on the desk.

"Collin," the older man said, clearing his throat, "I'm a lawyer by profession—but my nickname is 'Preacher Dick' . . ."

Collin gripped the arms of the chair tightly. He didn't know what was coming next. He was so afraid of messing up. And he wanted to feel clean inside again.

"Anyway, I think it's commendable—your change of heart,

that is. You're visibly sorry for the driving-while-intoxicated offense. I like that."

"Yes sir," Collin said thickly.

"I'll help you in court all I can, son. But there are some things I want you to do."

Collin felt a trickle of sweat run down his neck. "Yes, sir. Anything."

"First of all, I suggest you get that hair cut. You look like a sheep badly in need of shearing."

"Yes, sir."

"And I know where your family goes to church, but I think it'd be best for you if you tried my church. I'm not telling you where to worship, mind you. But I'm sure if you try my church once, you'll want to continue worshiping there."

"Uh—yes, sir," Collin said, reluctantly.

"And there's one more thing."

"Yes?"

"Have you ever taken Christ as your Lord?"

"I—uh—don't think so, sir."

Six months later, Collin lay in the darkness of his bed, unable to sleep. He cried out this prayer of desperation:

Jesus, I know I'm no good. But please help me. It's Preacher Dick—he's driving me crazy.

He's calling me up once a week. Making sure I go to Bible studies. And he picks me up for church on Sunday mornings and Wednesday nights.

And on the drives to church, he kind of cuts down my dad and brother. I know he thinks they're no good. He says the church my family goes to is too "liberal" and in the devil's hands. He really tears into my friends, too. He says they're *scum. I know my friends aren't perfect, but are they really* that *bad?*

There's all kinds of things about Preacher Dick that I kind of see when he drives me to church. Like—I'm sorry, Lord—but he's pretty mean, the things he says about other people.

But the hardest thing of all, Jesus, is all the rules he says I have to obey to make you happy. He says I've got to stay home on Friday nights. Bible study on Saturday night. I can't talk to this guy, or that girl. I can't drink this, but I can drink that. Can't watch this TV show, or listen to that radio station. Every day I try real hard, Lord, to obey all the rules—but I always end up breaking at least one.

If this is what being a Christian is, I don't know if I can stand it forever—because I can hardly stand it even one day. . . .

Collin didn't get the "amen" out before he started weeping. What should Collin do?

Other Voices:

"You'll get used to being a Christian. Just stick it out."

"Preacher Dick almost sounds like a cult leader to me. Tell him where to go."

"Preacher Dick's read his Bible his whole life. Who are you to question him?"

"Your religion's driving you crazy."

God's Voice:

A Christian, according to the Bible, is not a person who perfectly obeys a set of "Christian laws" on his or her own power:

But now we are discharged from the law [the condemnation of the Ten Commandments], dead to that which held us captive, so that we serve not under the old written code but in the new life of the Spirit. What then should we say? That the law is sin? By no means! (Romans 7:6–7a)

The Christian is a person whom Jesus Christ lives within

through the Holy Spirit. That Spirit helps us live a Christ-like life, because not one of us can live such a life on mere human power.

> Christ in you [is] the hope of glory. Him we proclaim, warning every man and teaching every man in all wisdom, that we may present every man mature in Christ. (Colossians 1:26–27)

> The Spirit helps us in our weakness. (Romans 8:26)

Your Voice:

1. Who is closer to being a biblical Christian—Preacher Dick, or Collin?
2. Does being a Christian mean you're perfect?
3. Did Preacher Dick show love to Collin?
4. Does *knowing* the fact that Christ lives within a Christian to help him or her live a Christ-like life change your concept of Christianity?
5. How can you enjoy true Christian freedom?
6. There's something called "jail-house religion"—a desperate person suddenly "repents" to look better in the eyes of the court. Does Collin have "jail-house religion"?
7. What does it mean that we are "discharged from the law"? Does it mean we can do whatever we want?
8. What positive value does the law have in our lives?
9. Should we believe everything a person says, just because they are called "Christian" or "spiritual"?
10. Are you a Christian according to the Bible's definition?

Other Books by Dallas Groten

Winning Isn't Always First Place
Will the Real Winner Please Stand
Ordinary Champions